MAKING SCHOOLS
WORK

A Vision for College and Career Ready Learning

WILLARD R. DAGGETT

Copyright © 2016 by International Center for Leadership in Education, Inc.
All rights reserved.
Published by International Center for Leadership in Education, Inc.
Printed in the U.S.A.

ISBN-13: 978-1-328-01231-9
ISBN-10: 1-328-01231-X

International Center for Leadership in Education, Inc.
1587 Route 146
Rexford, New York 12148
(518) 399-2776
fax (518) 399-7607
www.LeaderEd.com
info@LeaderEd.com

1 2 3 4 5   0014   20 19 18 17
4510003724   ABCDE

Dedication

To all of the teachers and administrators with whom
I have had the privilege to work, who are focused on preparing
students for their future rather than being anchored in the
instruction of the past: I salute you.

Contents

Acknowledgments

While I am listed as the sole author of this book, it is the collective work of a team of highly competent and dedicated professionals.

As with my most recent book, *Rigor, Relevance, and Relationships in Action*, I had a partner in conceptualizing, organizing, and writing *Making Schools Work*. Tim Weller is that partner. As a former reporter and editor with several of our nation's newspapers, including *USA Today* and *The Detroit News*, Tim did the majority of the writing on this book. "Thank you" is too mild an expression of gratitude for all that he did to bring the book from concept to completion.

Lynn Van Dine, who is also a former reporter and editor for both *USA Today* and *The Detroit News*, reviewed and revised the draft and final copy of the book. Her keen eye for detail and her perspective as a seasoned reporter were invaluable.

Peter McBride and I have worked on many books together over the past 30 years. A former head of Southwestern Publishing, Pete has guided me through writing dozens of textbooks and popular press books on education. Once again, his guidance has been incomparable.

Ray McNulty, my longtime advisor, friend, and Dean of the School of Education at Southern New Hampshire University, wrote the Foreword to this book, encouraging us to find the passion to take action and play our part in moving our country's education toward true college and career readiness for *all*.

A special thank you goes to my editors, Kris Ross and Kelly Griego. Editing my writing is a task few would want to tackle or have the ability to do. Kris and Kelly did a great job. Thank you, both.

Finally, to Dr. Linda Lucey, our Executive Director of Program Design, who oversaw the entire process: my hat's off to you. Guiding the team who worked on the book was like herding a group of cats. Great job, Linda!

Foreword

Why Listen?

Hardly a day goes by without someone discussing the topic of education and how to fix the public schools in our nation. Everyone seems to have a solution that, if implemented, would revolutionize learning for all and drive the cost of our systems back to that of the 1950s. Yes, that is what we hear on the streets, in bars, on planes, at neighborhood parties, and in our town halls, state capitals, and Washington, D.C. There is clearly no shortage of talk and ideas on how to bring education for all into the twenty-first century.

Few, if any, sharing their thoughts and ideas have had the actual experience necessary to help shape their thinking as has Bill Daggett. I met Bill while I was at the Gates Foundation leading work on secondary school reform. I was fortunate in my career as a teacher, principal, superintendent, and commissioner of education in Vermont to join the Foundation and work with some amazing schools and leaders. Many of these schools were faced with significant economic, educational, and poverty-driven challenges, yet these schools and their students achieved and even soared. There was much to learn from these schools. That's where my Bill Daggett story begins.

Bill and his team were eager to pop open the hood and get deep into the inner workings of these incredibly successful and rapidly improving schools. I was so excited about the work that I even left the Gates Foundation to join them!

So off Bill and I went with our colleagues at the International Center for Leadership in Education and the Successful Practices Network to identify the most rapidly improving schools in our nation and look deeply at their DNA.

Bill has written much and spoken often about the important lessons we have learned from these schools, always drawing connections to his deep career observations from the past 25 years crisscrossing the globe and meeting with educators, business leaders, and elected officials. He addresses this topic often because certain details of the message are always changing. This is because Bill and rapidly improving schools understand that as times change, education must also change.

In Part One of this book, Bill takes a deep dive into the vision driving decisions at today's most rapidly improving schools. At its core, the vision that these schools share is future focused, which requires emphasis on why students need to be both "College and Career Ready" when they graduate. Part Two provides pragmatic frameworks and resources to help you transition away from a twentieth-century rules, regulations, and traditions-based model and into an increasingly student-centered, technologically driven, information-based model— where culture trumps strategy and vision drives decisions!

So why listen? Well, if the paragraphs above haven't convinced you to take Bill's words seriously, let me share a few other points about him. I have been a professional educator since 1973, meaning I have talked with, shared space with, taught with, and created with a vast number of educators all looking to do what is right for our students, and none has more passion for our students than Bill Daggett. Yes, Bill cares about educators, but he lives to help students. And not just some of our students—he wants *all* students to succeed. Bill is not just about words and ideas; Bill is about action. He works tirelessly to ensure that all students get what they need to be successful and to feel valued, and he won't rest until we meet that goal.

Read his words and find the passion he exhibits to take action and grow the schools and educators we need to *make schools work* for our children so that they can truly be college and career ready.

Raymond J. McNulty
Dean, School of Education, Southern New Hampshire University
Author, *It's Not Us Against Them: Creating the Schools We Need*

Part One

A Vision for Schools That Work

Those of you who know me know I've built a career on urging educators to consider tomorrow as they plan for today. When I was working as a business and career/technical education teacher in New York State in the 1970s, I organized a group of educators to fight for more computer classes in K–12 public education. We could see that computer technologies were going to transform the future. And if we wanted our students to be successful in that future, they were going to have to be computer literate.

Since then, computer technologies have taken us places I never could have imagined. And so much faster than I could have imagined! We have artificial intelligence powering smartphones to which we give commands. In certain technology hubs, it's possible to spot a self-driving car on the roads. With one little device, we can control all manner of electronics and functions in our homes while vacationing on the other side of the globe.

These examples only prove how critical it is for us as educators always to be future-focused as we make instructional plans. How rapidly these technologies are changing all areas of life only makes it that much more urgent.

Throughout my career, I've had the great privilege of speaking with thousands of educators across the country and around the world. I also work closely with the nation's most rapidly improving schools. I've always wanted to know what it is they think, say, feel, and do that allows them to make such effective improvements so quickly—so that we can share their experiences and insights with you—our country's educators, school board members, parents, and business leaders.

As the circumstances in our world change, so too do the strategies and tactics of the nation's most rapidly improving schools. These schools understand that how to deliver education that will prepare students for *their* futures is not static. They evolve because they have to keep pace with what's evolving around us.

Over the past couple of years, I've noticed that those educators, schools, and districts making the biggest advances toward excellent twenty-first-century instruction share a mindset and similar core values that are foundational to their vision.

First, they have a growth mindset. They believe that they can rise to the occasion of innovating, originating, and creating new ideas, systems, strategies, and tactics to meet the needs of the students in their classrooms right now. Their minds, and thus their ideas, do not stay stuck in old thinking or past ideas. Instead, they remain open and support each other through fresh thinking and bold action.

Second, they hold a vision for their districts, schools, and classrooms that is based on shared core values. They see children as the future and the hope. They see their jobs as emphasizing career skills just as much as they emphasize academic skills. They know that instruction is not about teaching, but about making sure students learn. They understand they have a responsibility to teach students to *do*, not just to know. Working with their colleagues to prepare students for the world they will inherit, they think and function like entrepreneurs. And they approach budgeting with the ultimate growth mindset so that their financial plans support their vision, not the other way around.

These vision-sustaining "core values," as I call them, are the focus of this book.

In the first seven chapters, I make the case for why we need a new vision for our education system, followed by an exploration of the six core values driving the visions of the nation's most rapidly improving schools.

In Chapters Eight, Nine, and Ten, I offer practical frameworks and resources so you and your teams can begin implementing vision and across-the-board changes today.

A future focus underpins the core values. And a future focus means knowing what's in the pipeline so you know what skills your students need to hone today for success tomorrow. At the International Center for Leadership in Education (ICLE), the company I founded in 1991, we are always scanning employment statistics and trends and reading about the changing labor market. We do this so we can keep a handle on which skills are becoming obsolete and which will be in demand in the future. We also keep our fingers on the pulse of trends we see emerging in and around education that will impact how we must teach. In Chapter Eight, I share all these trends so that you can begin incorporating them into your classrooms today.

In Chapters Eight and Nine, I introduce the Rigor/Relevance Framework® and the Daggett System for Effective Instruction (DSEI)—frameworks my team and I at ICLE developed to transform districts and schools into epicenters of twenty-first-century instruction and thinking.

Before districts and schools set out to enact bold change, they must create a culture that supports bold change. *Culture trumps strategy*. This is the launching point of DSEI. From there, before districts and schools can begin making bold decisions, they must have a vision that can serve as a yardstick against which all decisions are measured. *Vision drives decisions*.

The six core values in this book have guided the visions that have moved so many schools closer to our collective goal: preparing *all* of our students for success in life and careers in the world they will live in.

As I write this book in 2016, the world feels turned upside down. We are in the midst of dramatic changes and facing strong socioeconomic headwinds and national challenges. What is relevant for us educators is that we prepare our students to do what life will demand of them: find solutions to very large problems. We all stand to lose or gain with their ability to do so.

How will we mold and shape our students to be the originators, thinkers, innovators, doers, and game changers when it's their turn at bat? Join me in learning how to get in the minds and adopt the vision of the educators doing just that.

Chapter One

A Foundation for Future-Focused Learning

L et me say this out of the gate: I am optimistic about our future. As individuals, educators, and a nation, I am hopeful. We are not without our challenges. We're living in a moment of change from all corners of our world. We are inundated with news, statistics, and anecdotes that remind us every day that this ain't your dad's world. And given your age, this might not even feel like *your* world.

Change is unnerving. But at certain points in time, it can allow— even demand—exciting opportunities to be bold. This is one of those times, because we *need* change. We are staring down some difficult socioeconomic circumstances that will compel valiant action and dramatic change.

All this change swirling around us is relevant for three reasons.

First, as we all know, technology has fundamentally transformed our day-to-day lives. Technology has influenced or upended almost everything: how we communicate, how we work and collaborate, how we shop, how we spend our leisure time, and on and on. Behind all these changes are changes in industries and careers. Technology has in many ways been like a wrecking ball to the status quo, knocking down legacy industry after legacy industry, and this effect isn't slowing down anytime soon. The careers that will be available to our students—and the skills needed for them—will be very different from the ones that were available to us when we graduated.

Second, all these technology-driven shifts and disruptions in careers have had direct impacts on the economy. The evolving job market is colliding with mounting socioeconomic headwinds, and each is having an exacerbating effect on the other. Fixing our ever-serious socioeconomic challenges will be one of the most important things we as a nation achieve in the coming decades. Our economic viability depends on it.

Third, it is our students who will have to confront and navigate through these socioeconomic headwinds, create successful careers and a vibrant economy despite them, and dream up the solutions to the challenging conditions we as a country face. I have full faith that they can. And I have full faith that our educators—some of the most important people in our country today—can help get them ready to take the call.

What the Typewriter Tells Us

I graduated from high school in 1964. One of the classes my contemporaries and I took senior year was typing. We practiced on manual machines the first half of the year, then switched to electric models in the second half.

One of the skills our teacher attempted to teach us was how to make copies on the typewriter. To do this, you took a piece of carbon paper—a thin, dark sheet of carbon—and slipped it, shiny side down, between two sheets of typing paper. When you started typing on the first sheet, the letters and words would transfer the carbon to the second sheet. Pretty amazing! (Trust me, it was at the time.) Just one problem— if you made a typing error, you either had to start over or try to erase your mistake somehow.

Quick confession: even though I've spent most of my adult life in public education, I was then, and remain today, a terrible speller. Can you imagine what my copies looked like when I misspelled practically every other word? Sometimes I think it was a miracle I graduated.

For a century, the typewriter and carbon paper were considered state of the art. Both were standard office equipment that, believe it or not, brought big efficiency gains to the workplace.

Let me pass along an endearing story that puts the change in technology into perspective. One day, my wife, Bonnie, and one of our grandsons, Reagan, age eight at the time, were in her home office looking for something. Bonnie told him to look under the typewriter. Reagan was puzzled.

"What's a typewriter?" he asked. When Bonnie explained what it was, Reagan wanted to see how it worked. She demonstrated, and Reagan just started laughing. "Why would anyone use something like that?" he wondered.

It's a humorous question to those of us who once relied on these typewriters to get work done. It's also a poignant question. Why *would* anyone use something like that? It's inefficient. It's unforgiving and rigid. It's clunky and cumbersome. It makes you go to it. In other words, it's steeped in and of the past.

With technologies at their fingertips that are nimble, eliminate steps, save time, and make lives easier in ways our parents could never have dreamed of, this digital generation knows only speed and efficiency. What my grandson's question reveals is that our children growing up in the twenty-first century have an intuitive knack and preference for the most efficient solutions and means to them. This is great news. A habit of and intuitive need for efficient, logical solutions will serve today's children well once they take the mantle as tomorrow's problem solvers and innovators.

I am optimistic about today's students and their futures.

The typewriter story also reveals two more points that every educator today needs to be aware of. One is a reminder of how many jobs have been destroyed as technologies have advanced and increased efficiency so rapidly to a point of rendering entire products, services, and industries obsolete. This will only keep happening.

The second is how different teaching has become. Teaching students how to make copies on carbon paper is far different from teaching them how to become problem solvers, innovators, thinkers, and doers. And let's be honest, it's harder. Not impossible. It just means that educators have to have a clear vision and plan in place, working toward a clear goal.

That goal is molding *all* of our students to understand and know how to create successful careers and self-sufficient lives in a world we can't yet imagine—one where their smartphones will be typewriters to the next generation. To get there, we must follow the lead of those educators blazing this path forward and adopt some new core values. We have no choice.

Technology and Jobs: A Complicated Relationship

The call to change our schools is urgent. It's as urgent as it's ever been. The pace of change in our world is only getting faster. The longer we take to get started, the harder the work becomes for us. Let's dive in now, before our challenges get that much more difficult to fix.

I don't need to tell you how radically technology has changed the way we work and live. Most of us remember what it was like for us or our parents to book travel through a travel agent. Or to deposit checks at the bank's drive-through window. Or to page through the phone book to find businesses and call them on our rotary phones. What matters for us educators is the wreckage that changing technologies leave in their wake.

Until about 1970, the median income for all workers showed a healthy, consistent increase. Thanks to new technologies and new overseas markets, the rising tide lifted almost every boat from about 1950 to 1970.

Then something happened. A large segment of the workforce was cast off from this economic expansion.

As in the early twentieth century, when the assembly line and mechanization wiped out low-skill jobs, in the late twentieth and early twenty-first century, advancements in automation and Internet technology came after middle-skill, middle-wage jobs. Researchers from Oxford University predict that 47 percent of all U.S. jobs will be automated within the next 10-20 years (Frey & Osborne, 2013).

"Many people have heard of Moore's Law," says Jeff Brown, technology executive and editor for Bonner & Partners. "Every 18 months computer processing power doubles. And each time, we get extraordinary improvements in technology. This has been going on since the late '60s.

"In the early stages of exponential growth—say, the first 20 doublings—the change isn't dramatic at all. But when you get to the twenty-sixth doubling, you reach the 'elbow' of the curve. And after that, the progress shoots straight up" (Satterfield, 2015).

Put another way, computers and robots do not need to be paid. They don't need health insurance. They don't get sick or take vacations. And they perform consistently at high levels of efficiency and precision. It's inevitable that as automation technologies become more mainstream and affordable, companies will choose them for cost savings and quality assurance.

New technologies have already displaced entire categories of factory-based labor, which were historically middle-wage jobs. These workers, with mostly limited or unspecialized skills, have found themselves unemployed or with stagnating wages as technology has cheapened the value of their skills. These workers are usually qualified for only a limited scope of jobs, and those jobs continue to disappear. As technologies have helped higher-earning workers become more efficient in their roles, these once middle-class, now-disenfranchised workers have had no choice but to take lower-skilled—and lower-paying—jobs.

Today, a driving force behind automation is artificial intelligence. AI, as it is commonly called, is the development of computer systems able to perform tasks that normally require human intelligence, such as visual perception, writing algorithms, speech recognition, decision-making, and translation between languages. AI already exists in our personal lives. Apple's "Siri," "Google Now," Microsoft's "Cortana," and Facebook's "M" have become indispensable virtual assistants for many people.

Today, the holy grail of AI—creating software that comes close to mimicking human intelligence—remains just out of reach. But companies like Google, Facebook, Microsoft, and IBM are spending billions trying to develop machines that will possess human intelligence and common sense.

With the Industrial Revolution, technology brought productivity gains and physical support to manual laborers. As mechanization technologies advanced, they eventually replaced human laborers. In its earliest forms, AI brought efficiencies to knowledge workers, who have historically been higher paid. Now AI is threatening to replace even some of them. In short, if an AI algorithm can be written to do a job, that job will be gone.

The Missing Middle

As more companies choose computerized help over human labor, the decline in middle-wage jobs will become dramatic. It's happening already.

In December 2015, the Pew Research Center issued a sobering report showing that America's middle class had shrunk from 61 percent of the population to 49 percent (Pew Research Center, 2015). That's a stunning—if predictable—statistic.

Pew defines middle class as an adult earning two-thirds to double the national median wage. That means a three-person household would have to earn between $42,000 and $126,000 each year to be considered middle class. Pew found middle-income wealth plunged 28 percent from 2001 to 2013. In addition, the percentage of low-income households increased to 29 percent. In most industries, the report showed that the number of workers in the "middle" tier decreased while workers in the "upper" and "lower" tiers increased.

After sifting through Pew's numbers, you can arrive at only one conclusion: the rich are getting richer, the poor are getting poorer, and the middle class is getting squeezed at both ends.

For educators, this trend is critical because the purpose of public education has always been to prepare students to realize their full potential. For many, that meant entering the middle class—a middle class that today is vanishing at an alarming rate.

I've said it before and I'll say it again: the world is changing at an ever-increasing pace. Technology continues to profoundly change the way we live and work.

Our National Debt

Our national debt—now approaching $20 trillion, slightly higher than the 2015 GDP—has climbed quickly in recent years. That should have triggered some economic pain. Yet we're relatively pain free. There's a reason for that: The Federal Reserve, the central bank of the United States, has kept interest rates close to zero for years.

I don't want to get too deep into the economic weeds. But near-zero interest rates are relevant for a few reasons. By keeping benchmark interest rates near zero, the Federal Reserve is trying to encourage borrowing and spending to promote economic activity. When the Fed keeps the interest rate close to zero for years, it's implying, at least in part, that the economy is not strong enough to withstand higher rates. For context, except for the period from about 1970 to 2000, the rate has hovered around five percent *since 1820* (Irwin, 2015). If it rose to that historical norm now, interest on the national debt would be a trillion dollars a year.

Our country must meet its repayment obligations on the national debt. Failure to do so would mean default and all the economic ruin that would bring—a collapsing dollar, massive inflation, and spiking unemployment, not to mention the impact on international economies. To make matters worse, China owns about eight percent of our debt, or about $1.2 trillion.

The Demographic Tidal Wave (Crashing Down on Benefits)

America's 76.4 million baby boomers are starting to retire en masse— and beginning to tap into Social Security, Medicare, and Medicaid. That's about 24 percent of the entire U.S. population. The lobbying power of this group has been, and certainly will continue to be, phenomenal. They will not stand by idly if our political leaders even begin to think about cutting those programs.

As a lifelong educator, this troubles me. Here's why:

Paying for Social Security, Medicare, and Medicaid, coupled with paying interest on the national debt, will put tremendous pressure on public dollars—and schools could be severely impacted. Tax dollars fund schools, and voters have the final say. Voters don't get to decide the state or federal income tax rate—but they *do* get to vote on school taxes.

We're headed down a road on which public education might be the only discretionary budgeting area where people can lash out against high taxes.

Don't get me wrong. I believe we owe it to society to pay for Social Security, Medicare, and Medicaid. But these three programs—plus our interest payments on the national debt—now account for 71 percent of the federal budget. If interest rates climb, or if the Chinese decide to raise their rates on our loans, there will be no money left for much else.

Including schools.

Let's Be Honest About Where We Are

My role with the International Center for Leadership in Education (ICLE) gives me a bird's-eye view of our education system. I can say that, by and large, our schools are not keeping pace with all the changes happening around them. However, there are some trailblazers out there taking risks, experimenting, and trying to build the new vision for twenty-first-century learning.

You have picked up this book, which means you are a trailblazer at core. I ask you to answer this candidly: Are you doing your part to make the classrooms in your school or district capable of molding twenty-first-century professionals and problem solvers? Look around you. Do your classrooms look as they did when you were a student? Are your school days operating just as they did when you were young? What about your friends and colleagues at other schools? What do their schools look like?

What does your gut say about what our schools are doing in terms of modernizing? Are you doing enough? Anything at all?

For us to make the changes that our students deserve and our country needs, we must start first by being honest.

I believe our public education system is the best in the world, period. We educate *all* children. It is our combined commitment to equity and excellence that makes our schools the best.

That said, do we have the highest standards? We don't. Do we have the most relevant standards? We don't. Consequently, confidence in our pre-K-12 education system is eroding because we're just not preparing our students for the world they will inherit and the challenges they will be called on to tackle.

I will not mince words. If we continue to teach students under the twentieth-century model (which is arguably the nineteenth-century model, as that's when our desk rows and bell systems were created), our employment and economic issues will only get worse and more widespread. Why? Because the twentieth-century model produces people prepared for twentieth-century jobs, most of which have been wiped out by technology.

The negative effects will start to cascade. Graduates prepared for the older way of working will fail to find careers that allow them to become self-sufficient. They will require more government assistance (read: your tax dollars). We are fortunate to live in a nation that can provide assistance for its people in need. But we can see where this vicious cycle could become an unsustainable economic path.

If we keep going down this path, eventually public education will come under financial threat. We can address both equity and excellence only because we can fund it—for now.

It's been more than 30 years since the National Commission on Excellence in Education issued the landmark report *A Nation at Risk: The Imperative for Educational Reform*. The report concluded that our school system was failing to provide an education that would create a competitive workforce. It made waves in 1983, and it still resonates today. It famously stated: "If an unfriendly foreign power had attempted to impose on America the mediocre educational performance that exists today, we might well have viewed it as an act of war. As it stands, we have allowed this to happen to ourselves."

When this report was written, the gap between the skills our students would need to succeed in careers and what they were learning in school was already wide. In terms of our education system at large, little has changed since then. Relative to what has changed in every other area of life, that gap is now better called a crevasse.

The key purpose of education—at least to my way of thinking—is to prepare students for the future. Education must *prepare our students to know what to do when they don't know what to do.* We need to prepare them for an increasingly unpredictable future.

Yet our focus all too often is on preparing students for the next grade level. We simply haven't adjusted to what is happening around us.

Ask yourself again: Have you and your colleagues begun to take the bold steps forward to instruct students for the twenty-first century? And if you haven't yet, why not? What are you waiting for? For things to get worse?

A Growth Mindset: A Prerequisite to Change

If you're going to have the difficult dialogues, you—and every person you have them with—must do so with a growth mindset. Otherwise, what's the point? What's the point of honestly appraising where you and your schools and districts are versus where you need to go if you can't figure out how to get there? Getting there requires having a growth mindset.

If we have these candid conversations with a fixed mindset, we will not be able to see beyond the status quo. Even if we didn't recognize it yet, we would default to the same solutions, systems, and structures in which we are stuck. A fixed mindset guarantees doubling down on the past.

But educating students today should be about their future. To get there, we must have a growth mindset. We must believe we are capable of changing, adapting, thinking differently and from new angles. We must believe we are capable of being imaginative, creative, original, and flexible as we look for new solutions to old problems. We must believe we are capable of persevering despite the obstacles certain to come up as we boldly forge a new path forward for education.

We must all have a growth mindset.

Before you and your colleagues roll up your sleeves and get to work, get in a growth mindset. Google Carol Dweck's work and the difference between a growth mindset and a fixed mindset. Develop mantras for a growth mindset and repeat them in advance of every meeting. Commit to a growth mindset, and recommit every day.

Six Core Values for Vision and Change

Part Two of this book includes frameworks and resources to help you and your teams begin making changes today. In Chapter Eight, you will find emerging trends and current employment data that should factor into future-focused instructional plans. The Rigor/Relevance Framework® follows in Chapter Nine and is an invaluable tool for confirming that curriculum, instruction, and assessment all address both knowledge acquisition and knowledge application.

Chapter Ten provides a detailed overview of the Daggett System for Effective Instruction (DSEI). DSEI is a systemwide approach for rethinking and remodeling entire districts and schools to point toward instructional effectiveness and student achievement goals aligned to a shared vision. The framework encompasses the three segments of Organizational Leadership, Instructional Leadership, and Teaching. Each segment has elements, or strategies, to systematically bring vision-aligned change to each one and, thus, ultimately the entire system.

The first element of organizational leadership, or the first point that must be thought through as leaders begin systemic change, is creating a culture of change. Anyone who's heard me speak knows one of my favorite lines: *Culture trumps strategy.* Before a school can innovate, improve, and make broad, productive changes, it must adopt a culture to support such changes. Strategies are mission critical. But without a culture to support the strategies, they are dead on arrival. Culture trumps strategy.

The next element is establishing a shared vision. To do this, leaders must ask guiding questions to define with their teams what is essential to twenty-first-century instructional effectiveness for student success. What results are core values that form a vision that will become the yardstick against which all decisions and plans are measured? Does this plan align to our vision? Will this action help realize our vision? If the answer is ever "no," it's not a step worth taking. *Vision drives decisions.*

Each year, I get the exciting opportunity to observe and analyze the nation's most rapidly improving schools. For decades, I've been sharing with you all the revolutionary steps these schools take to reap remarkable results. This book is an opportunity to discuss my latest observations from the field. Specifically, I'm sharing six core values driving visions at schools effecting rapid change that's paying off with tangible, positive student achievement gains.

In Part One of this book, I ask you to consider six core values for a vision that will help prepare students to thrive in the world that awaits them. More and more of us are realizing that we don't need just more easy tweaks or more of the past in new shoes. We need a complete overhaul. To get there, we must cultivate the culture to enable it, and then define a vision to realize it.

The six core values of schools doing their part to revolutionize the system are:

- **Core Value 1: Students are the hope of our future.** Educators are not glorified babysitters, watching over students five days a week, six hours a day, 180 days a year. Educators are key influencers in the lives and futures of students. Schools must develop a system in which we both see and treat students as the hope of the future, not merely a responsibility for the time being. This means guiding students to understand their roles in the future and believe in their ability to thrive in them.
- **Core Value 2: Career ready must be on equal footing with college ready.** Educators must develop a system that outfits students with career skills—not just academic skills—so that students are career- and future-ready, where career readiness requires students to be creative, innovative, team-oriented, comfortable with ambiguity, and self-directed. Educators must also coach students through how to make wise and practical college decisions.
- **Core Value 3: The focus of instruction must be learning.** Educators must shift from a system focused on teaching to

a system focused on *learning*. Decisions must be made with learning, not instructional, goals in mind. This reminds us that students—not adults—should be at the center of all of our decisions. It also reminds us the critical role data plays in revealing true learning—or the absence of it.

- **Core Value 4: We must teach our students to *do*.** Educators must develop a system focused on what students need to do, not just what they need to know. We must help students gain comfort and confidence taking action with knowledge, and we must help them see that if they hope to do, they must have and create opportunities for doing. After all, being successful in careers means winning the opportunity to put their knowledge to work for reward. The bedrock to doing and empowering action are twelve noncognitive Guiding Principles.

- **Core Value 5: Educators must think like entrepreneurs.** Economic growth is moving toward smaller, entrepreneurial businesses, and schools must reflect this shift by emulating their organizational structures and the mindsets of those who work in them. An entrepreneurial mindset is one that encourages openness, originality, agency, flexibility, and experimentation. In adopting this mindset, educators are primed for innovative solutions and ideas and will mirror to students the attitudes and behaviors their careers will require of them.

- **Core Value 6: Districts and schools must adopt zero-based budgeting.** Zero-based budgeting—an approach to budgeting according to future goals, not past patterns—is being adopted in the private sector and some pioneering schools. It is the ultimate growth-mindset method of budgeting. Traditional budgeting causes us to double down on the past, rather than consider a different future and the budget needed to realize it. Zero-based budgeting allows even the budget to align to vision.

What's the point of and power behind these core values? How do we use them to make the bold decisions we must to make our schools work for today's students—the hope of the future? The answers—and the spirit of rapidly improving schools—follow.

Chapter Two

Core Value 1: Students Are the Hope of Our Future

We as a nation are facing some strong economic headwinds, as I mentioned in Chapter One. I also mentioned that I am optimistic that we will find solutions to rise above them. But this will only be possible if we educators recognize one important fact: our students, the very children who sit before us every school day, are our hope.

If they are the hope, what are we teachers? We are the conduits.

While I don't want to belabor our economic woes, I do want to delve deeper into one aspect of them to drive home just how critical it is that we make sure all of our students can find good paying jobs and create successful, self-sufficient careers in this century. Not only must they do this for themselves, but they must do this, as you will see, for the sustainability of our economy.

The Government Support Spiral

Support ratio is an economic term that refers to ways the government supports its citizens. There are two kinds of support: direct government benefits and indirect government benefits.

We all receive indirect government benefits. For example, we drive on roads and highways that governments have built; our military protects and defends us from our enemies.

Direct government benefits mean the government is doing something for me personally—either giving me money or paying for something for me. Twenty-three percent of all Americans under the age of 18—74.2 million people—are receiving more direct government benefits than they pay in (U.S. Census Bureau, 2011). To this I say thank goodness, because these are all "our" children.

How do they receive direct government benefits? For most of those in this age group, it's through schooling, which is funded by local, state, and federal tax dollars. That is wonderful! But it is a lot of people.

Another group of people who typically receive more direct government support than they pay in are those age 65 and older. At that age, most Americans have left the workforce and are collecting Social Security, Medicare, and Medicaid. This is another 14.1 percent of the population, or 45 million people (U.S. Census Bureau, 2011).

Beginning in 1964, President Lyndon Johnson and Congress introduced the Great Society, a set of domestic programs designed to eliminate poverty and reduce racial injustice. In some ways, the Great Society resembled President Franklin D. Roosevelt's New Deal agenda, designed to pull the country out of the Great Depression. Medicare, Medicaid, and federal education funding, among others, are Great Society programs that continue to this day.

Take a close look at the following chart (Figure 1). It shows that in 1960, the population dynamics were such that there were more young people than old. Thus, the thinking was, there were plenty of younger folks who would age into the workforce and contribute productively to society, pay taxes, and fund social programs for the retired and underprivileged.

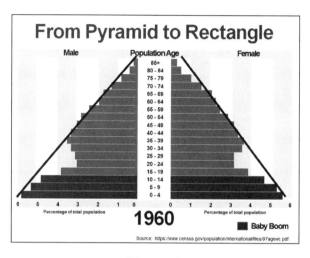

Figure 1

There were two assumptions driving the Great Society: that our population would remain a pyramid indefinitely, and that lifespan wouldn't budge much. But look what was happening by the 1990s (Figure 2): the baby boomers became America's prime workforce, and there were already more older people living well past 65.

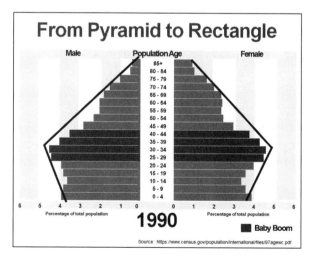

Figure 2

Today, our pyramid has morphed into a rectangle (Figure 3). The aging baby boomers are retiring from the workforce and tapping Social Security, Medicare, and Medicaid.

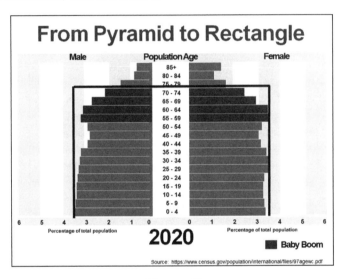

Figure 3

The number of people 65 and older will jump to 80 million by 2030 (Ortmann, Velkoff, & Hogan, 2014). They will be an incredible lobbying force. They will live longer, on average until 80. They will not allow the government to cut their benefits. In fact, many might say, "We want more."

Exacerbating our funding squeeze, 127 million working-aged Americans—or 39.7 percent of those in this 18-to-65 age group—are not working. They are not paying tax on income and some are receiving government support through Medicare, Medicaid, Social Security or college financial assistance. 127 million people!

In sum, 246 million Americans in total—that's 76.8 percent—are not working full time, and some are receiving, or have at one time received, government support.

There's one final group that I must add to the mix, and it's many of you reading this book. Public employees. Public employees, and certainly educators, are invaluable workers and essential contributors to this nation and its economy. Yet we must bear in mind that taxpayers are paying 100 percent of their salaries. They, mathematically, receive more in direct government paid salaries and benefits than they pay out through taxes. That's 22.4 million of you, or 7 percent of the total U.S. population.

What all of this analysis means, should our present economic trends persist, is that in the future, 91 percent, or 303.6 million people, will not be employed full time and will likely receive government assistance of some type, from Medicare to free public education.

In other words, only nine percent of Americans will be paying to support the remaining 91 percent. That is unsustainable.

The 91% are not—repeat: NOT—scamming the system.

The kids aren't taking advantage of the system; they're going to school. Retiring workers over 65 aren't taking advantage of the system; they're collecting the Social Security, Medicare, and Medicaid due them. Public employees are not taking advantage of the system; they are hard-working, contributing members of society who provide a wealth of indirect government benefits to their fellow citizens.

It's just not sustainable.

It's also important that we consider the larger implications this support spiral could have on the funding of public education.

Failure Is Not an Option

I've repeatedly mentioned how grateful I am that programs like Social Security, Medicare, and Medicaid exist. That's because it's personal.

I have a 97-year-old father without any other financial resources of his own. Social Security and Medicare keep him afloat.

My wife, Bonnie, and I have a daughter, Audrey, who is severely learning disabled and suffers from autism, and epilepsy. Audrey is 44 and will never live independently.

Social Security and Medicaid help her survive.

In both my dad's case and Audrey's, my wife and I are able to help support them. However, that is not the case with many families. Social Security, Medicare, and Medicaid are for many their only form of support.

We've got to take care of the neediest in this country, and Audrey and my father are just two of millions of examples. The only way we can continue to support our citizens and structures is through a strong economy where there is more tax revenue coming in than there are support expenses going out.

Hopefully by now it is clear why our students, those in our classrooms, are the hope of our future. They will be called on to become productive, contributing members of society. For our nation to sustain the prosperity we've long known and cherished, our students simply must be able to pay more into the system than they take out. They simply must have the skills that the twenty-first-century economy demands and rewards. They simply must know how to navigate the twenty-first-century career jungle. They simply cannot get left behind, armed with nothing more than outdated twentieth-century skills that are of little value in today's technology-driven world.

In my career, I've coached countless educators through dramatic, systemwide overhauls. I know something to be true of successful change initiatives: before asking people to change, you must tell them *why*. Our economic challenges and the role our students will play in confronting them is the why.

From there, I ask everyone to love their students more than they love their peers. This is, after all, about the students. And through them—the people they have the potential to become—it is about us, as a nation and as individuals. But they must come first.

As educators, we must be sure our students know what's being asked of them. And we must be sure they know we believe in them.

A Mindset of Optimism

Let's break this down into simple terms. If someone believes in us, we are more likely to do good and do well. If no one believes in us, well then we are likely to lower ourselves to meet those expectations. Faith in our own abilities motivates us to avoid disappointing those who have faith in us. We as educators must always remember this.

We cannot control the homes in which our students are raised. But we can balance any lack of optimism in them by bringing it—with full force—into our classrooms. I encourage you regularly to tell your students they are the hope. They will one day take their places as the leaders of this country, and we must make sure they believe they can do so triumphantly.

By constant reminders of this fact, students' brains will slowly rewire. By no means am I suggesting doom and gloom when explaining to students how crucial they are to building and sustaining a better future for all; this role is true of all of our students, no matter the moment in history. It's just to say that by talking in lofty terms about how all students are capable of more than they can imagine from their perch in the classroom, you will prime them to take on challenges with gusto. And there's evidence to back this up.

The Proof Is in the Self-Efficacy

Psychologist and former Stanford professor Albert Bandura is considered a foremost expert on self-efficacy, which is really just a fancy term for believing in one's self. Bandura defined self-efficacy as a person's belief that he or she can accomplish a specific task or goal. He was curious to know just how much believing that one can achieve a goal determines ability to do so. In 1977, he published his landmark report, "Self-Efficacy: Toward a Unifying Theory of Behavioral Change," that linked a belief in one's self to improved outcomes (Bandura, 1977).

In his research, Bandura found that a person's degree of self-efficacy affects how that person thinks, acts, and feels. He observed a direct correlation between self-belief and attitudes about potential, which then shaped the person's choices. People with high self-efficacy, Bandura found, view challenges as opportunities for mastery, not threats to be escaped. They take greater interest in more things and activities and demonstrate more engagement with them. And they also show an ability to bounce back quickly from bumps in the road, which, over time, fosters a comfort with taking calculated risks (Bandura, 1977).

On the other hand, those with low self-efficacy tend only to focus on the limits of their potential. They therefore do what they can to avoid what they see as challenges. They are quick to lose confidence amid setbacks. And they have a tendency to dwell on their mistakes and what they perceive to be the negative results of those mistakes.

By simply boosting their self-efficacy, Bandura proved, people are more likely to confront, even reach for, challenging tasks, persevere even if they stumble, and take positive action on their own behalf. These beliefs begin taking shape in childhood—*in our classrooms*—and continue to evolve throughout life. Not surprisingly, those who develop more self-efficacy in their childhood will have more later in life.

What can we educators do to cultivate a system of positive self-belief in our schools and classrooms? According to Bandura, there are four ways that people increase their self-efficacy, and we can bear each in mind as we plan instruction and learning.

The most effective way is probably the most obvious: mastery. The most surefire way for a student to believe he or she is capable is by achieving mastery of a subject through a task. Interestingly, those students who observe a peer achieve mastery also see an uptick in their own self-efficacy. Second, Bandura found that social modeling, or watching someone like ourselves succeed at something, tells us that we too possess the skills to accomplish something similar. While social modeling packs a smaller punch than mastery, it is worth considering how social modeling can be built into instruction.

The third way that we can promote self-efficacy is the lowest hanging fruit: social persuasion. Bandura found that people can be persuaded to believe in themselves. By merely being told that he or she has the skills and ability to achieve something, a person begins to believe it. Verbal affirmation can help cut through self-doubt and encourage students to try. Perhaps most interesting from Bandura's research on this point is that the negative impact of negative feedback can have a greater effect than the positive impact of positive feedback. It's an important reminder to make negative feedback constructive, not personal, and to couple it with positive affirmation.

Finally, our moods, emotions, and stress levels can influence how we feel about our ability to succeed in specific situations or moments. If we're stressed out, our self-efficacy might drop. If we're in a great mood, we might feel more confidence and capability than usual.

Stress can be channeled into focused energy. Anxiety can be channeled into enthusiasm. Fears can become opportunities for wisdom and embracing imperfection. So-called failures can be reframed as nothing more than real-time data. People who are in a bad mood can be nudged into a better one if they are asked to think about or talk about something they care about. (For those of you who know the Rigor/Relevance Framework®, which we'll go into in detail in Chapter Nine, I'm talking about relevance and personalization here.) What's key at this point is really *listening* to your students. Hear their fears, let them know you care, and reassure them that they are safe and unjudged in your classroom.

Build self-efficacy into your vision so that you are reminded always to look for opportunities to boost it in your students as you plan your instruction and interact with them. How can you give each student a moment to shine and succeed as classmates watch? What can you say or do to help them manage, maybe even counteract, their stresses, fears, or anxieties?

What can you say to students to let them know you believe in them? As we read, the simplest way to help students believe in themselves is to tell them that doing and achieving great things is within their reach. They are capable of learning deeply, improving step by step, stretching themselves, taking calculated risks, and persevering if things don't work out as planned. They are capable of dreaming big and realizing those dreams. But they might simply need to be told this—explicitly and often.

Remind your students they are the future and they are the hope. Remind them that one day, they will be at the helm of this nation. Tell them you believe they will take their positions as future leaders, innovators, doers, creators, thinkers, problem solvers, and game changers successfully and skillfully, so long as they believe it, too. Let them know you are confident in them so that they absorb it by proxy. Set a high bar because you know they can rise to meet it.

On that note, I am confident that you too can be the highly effective conduits our students need to enter into college, should they choose to go, and into the working world with lifelong learning skills and the capacity to take appropriate action in multiple, unpredictable circumstances. I am confident that you can reshape your thinking, rewire your brain to be open to creative solutions to old problems and collaborate with your peers to make your school work for this century's dynamics and challenges.

As Henry Ford said, "Whether you think that you can, or think that you cannot, you are usually right."

Chapter Three

Core Value 2:
Career Ready Must Be on Equal
Footing with College Ready

Miniature Robots Under the Hood

In January 2016, I had the privilege of meeting with senior executives from General Motors, BMW, and Kia. These men and women were gathered in Detroit for the North American International Auto Show, the biggest and most prestigious show of its kind in the country.

I left that meeting amazed and troubled. I learned that the auto industry's workforce, from manufacturing to service centers to dealerships, is undergoing profound change. Here's just one example of a crucial job that's about to change: automotive technician.

Just about every Career and Technology Education program in this country has an auto tech program.

Today's cars contain anywhere from a few hundred to as many as a thousand data points that their internal computers monitor. What's happening today is that the auto industry is focused on prevention. For example, Ford's renowned racing car, the GT, contains 50 sensors that generate 100 gigabytes of data per hour and feed 28 microprocessors, which control everything from tire pressure to door latches. The car spits out more than 10 million lines of code, about 8 million more than an F-22 fighter jet, according to Henry Ford III, marketing manager of Ford Performance, Ford Motor Co.'s racing division.

The executives shared with me that through the use of nanotechnology, they believe that in the next five years auto manufacturers will be able to embed miniature robots in their cars. When the onboard computer identifies a potential problem, these miniature robots will fix the problem. Wow!

They also predict these miniature devices will be able to fix up to 80 percent of all mechanical and electronic problems in a car, without the owner ever having to bring it in for service. These embedded computers and miniature robots will monitor your car continuously. Wow again!

But think about the implications for the auto industry—and for our auto tech classes. This will change what everyone in the auto tech field will have to know and be able to do. The auto mechanic of the future will need deep skills in data analytics and statistics. This isn't your father's auto tech program! Teachers in these programs will need a completely different set of skills than they have now to remain relevant.

In the twentieth century, before Internet technologies turned everything we knew upside down, there was little difference between preparing students for college and careers. The skills required to get to and excel in college and those required to excel in careers were almost entirely the same.

In terms of the Rigor/Relevance Framework®, the twentieth century required Quads A/C skills. In other words, the twentieth-century economy was built on specific knowledge and area expertise that was applied to predictable circumstances. Careers often remained confined to one focus, one silo, one department. Thus, the college prep model of teaching—where knowledge is gathered through and applied to one discipline—sufficiently prepared students for careers back in the day.

But in the near future, there will be tiny robots under the hood of your car. They will recognize problems even before you do. They will fix them. And they will make it so you can take fewer trips to the auto repair shop. If you do need to take in your car, odds are that the "mechanic" will look at your car's computer code just as frequently, if not more often, than he or she will look under your car's hood. Thus, today's careers require Quadrant B/D critical thinking, creativity, and flexible knowledge application to unpredictable situations.

Four-year college remains important, appropriate, and affordable for many students. But not for all. Regardless of whether a student chooses to attend college, our ultimate goal as educators remains the same: we are aiming to get students into successful, self-sufficient lives, which usually comes by way of a career.

Today, college is more and more just one choice among many on the road to success. It's time we recognize that our twentieth-century instructional model simply won't cut it for twenty-first-century career preparation. We must figure out how to promote the academics that underpin "career ready" to be on equal footing with the academics that underpin "college ready."

College Today: A Blind Assumption and a Broken Promise

Within public education, ingrained assumptions are at work every minute of the day. Consider one of our most ingrained beliefs: a four-year college degree is a passport to success in career and life. It is true that a college degree benefits many students, and some graduates earn significantly more money than students who don't attend or graduate. But let's take a deeper look.

To be blunt, I believe for many of our students a bachelor's degree has become a false premise and a broken promise. College is no longer the guaranteed gateway to a good job that will equip a graduate for lifelong self-sustainability. Neither is the assumption, at least in terms of employment and being economically independent, that more college is better than less college.

A Tennessee study showed that the average salary of the state's graduates of two-year colleges is higher than four-year college graduates (American Institutes for Research, 2012). Why? Soaring demand for workers in technology fields. Moreover, the cost of earning a four-year or advanced degree has risen, in many cases, beyond any reasonable assessment of return on investment.

College graduates in 2011 were more likely to be underemployed as waiters, waitresses, bartenders, and food-service helpers than as engineers, physicists, chemists, and mathematicians combined, according to data reported by the Associated Press (Weissman, 2012). Many of these underemployed college graduates find themselves trapped in temporary jobs "until a real one comes along." They cling to false hope and are crippled by student loan debt.

In 2015, college graduates took on the most student debt in history. The class of 2015 graduated with $35,051 in student debt on average, according to an analysis from Mark Kantrowitz, the publisher of Edvisors.com, a website that provides information to students and parents about college costs and financial aid. That's about $2,000 more than that of 2014 graduates, though the percentage of students graduating with debt remained constant at about 70 percent.

In *Most Likely to Succeed: Preparing Our Kids for the Innovation Era*, Tony Wagner, an expert-in-residence at Harvard University's Innovation Lab, explains that not only are graduates in debt, but they are underprepared for the workforce.

"We hear from employers regularly about how ill-prepared graduates are, even graduates from elite colleges, to take on workplace responsibilities. How creativity and imagination have been schooled out of them. How they seem to be allergic to unstructured problems. How they seek constant micromanagement and the workplace equivalent of a daily, even hourly, grade" (Wagner, 2015).

As educators, isn't it our job to cultivate critical thinking skills, encourage creativity, nurture life skills, and instill confidence in our students? One could argue that these qualities are—college degree or not—the true path to success.

Not every student can, will, or should—for whatever reason—go to college. However, our young people deserve the opportunities to learn and develop the abilities, mindsets, the "I can" optimism, and the confidence to reach their highest potential as individuals in becoming successful, responsible, self-reliant adults and citizens who contribute to the betterment of society.

Majors Matter

For those who do go to college, they will get the highest return on their investment if they intentionally gain in-demand skills. This means what they major in matters. Those who select majors relevant to the real world will leave their college campuses with a competitive edge and higher earning power.

Let's compare the ten most common majors at four-year colleges in the United States in 2014 to the top ten majors in ten of the next most industrialized nations of the world.

Top 10 College Majors United States	Top 10 College Majors Other Industrialized Nations
Business	Business
General Studies	Engineering and Technology
Social Science and History	Computer and Information Science
Psychology	Health Care
Health Care	Education
Education	Social Science and History
Visual and Performing Arts	Communications and Journalism
Engineering and Technology	Visual and Performing Arts
Communications and Journalism	Psychology
Computer and Information Science	General Studies

What do these countries know that we don't? Do you think a general studies major today can live a self-sufficient life? How about a social science and history major? Maybe they will, but it's a tough road to travel compared to many other professions—unless they plan to pursue teaching or go on to graduate school to complete a degree that will lead to successful employment. Few do, and those who do drive themselves deeper into debt with additional loans.

Judging by all this data, our secondary schools and colleges don't understand what students need today and aren't providing the guidance that the students need to be successful in college so that, should they go, they can be successful in careers.

Are you telling your students, no matter their present grade, that what they major in matters, if and when they attend college? Are you pushing them to consider those majors that will provide them with skills that are in demand once they're out of college? Are you urging them to be optimistic *and* practical? Focused on the future?

It's not enough to help our students get to college. We must also help them use that precious time—that ever-more-expensive time—wisely. That is part of the process of and our duty in putting career ready on equal footing with college ready.

The other part is understanding what a career is.

What Does It Mean to Be Prepared for a Career?

Preparing students for careers is not the same as preparing them for a job. Career and tech education prepares students for jobs. College prep is focused on preparing students for success in higher education. Preparing students for a career is significantly different from preparing them for either a job or college.

Last century, when many workers landed their first significant jobs, they often stayed with that same employer until they retired. An employee would go to work for a large company, which provided a stable of benefits to entice the employee to stay for the long haul. The employee, in turn, felt loyal to the company and willing and wanting to climb the ladder. The ladder was straight, and what the employee needed to do to climb to each new rung was straightforward. Decades later, the employee retired with a pension and retiree healthcare benefits waiting for him or her like a carrot—or a pot of gold—at the end of a linear career path.

Not so today. Many of the industries and larger companies that dominated the twentieth-century economy have gotten the technology treatment. They've been knee-capped by technology, which has done all sorts of damage. In some cases, industries have been all but wiped out. (How often do you call your stockbroker these days? Or your travel agent?) In other cases, jobs have been shipped overseas. (Customer service, anyone?) In yet other cases, industries and companies are desperately trying to figure out how to adapt to the technology-driven economy, or else. (Good luck, newspapers and cable companies.)

With budgets under pressure from rapidly changing economic forces, payroll has been reduced (Craver, 2015) and several traditional company benefits, like pensions and retiree healthcare, have shrunk or disappeared (Brandon, 2014). What's more, many companies today avoid hiring people full time to get around having to pay benefits. Can't afford to provide healthcare benefits? Cut employee hours (Terhune, 2013).

Yet scores of new companies have cropped up and embraced technology as an opportunity to seize. These younger, entrepreneurial outfits entice employees less with the traditional benefits of yesteryear than with innovative, more cost-effective benefits, like a flexible workweek, opportunities to telecommute, or on-site wellness programs, to name some (IFEBP.org, 2014).

Employees trade company loyalty for the thrilling opportunity to work in a fast-paced environment where leadership is distributed, innovation and agency are expected, and interdisciplinary collaboration is the norm. At these companies, they can gather key skills and experience—to make them that much more qualified for their next gig.

These companies purposefully remain nimble, as they regularly iterate and pivot to adapt to the changing technologies and economic forces around them. This means career paths are murky at best and that far more employees cycle in and out as business models evolve and a company needs change.

In today's dynamic workplace, longevity with one company that was the model in the twentieth century is a quaint notion. The U.S. Bureau of Labor Statistics reports that the average worker now holds 10 different jobs before his or her fortieth birthday (U.S. Bureau of Labor Statistics, 2015). Forrester Research, a marketing and technology company, predicts that today's youngest workers will hold 12–15 jobs during their lifetimes (Experience.com, 2016).

Today's workers need the skills that the market demands and values, as well as the adaptability, creativity, flexibility, and perseverance to not just navigate a career path, but to build a career portfolio. At least that's how Donna Harris—the clever millennial entrepreneur who founded start-up incubator and seed funder 1776—describes careers today (Pennington, 2013). When the linear career path has also gotten the technology treatment, workers are left to build a career portfolio—a collection of different experiences that each individual must construct in a way that comes together well and can be pitched to a prospective employer.

The Career Readiness Partner Council, formed in 2012, is a group of leaders from national education and workforce organizations seeking to clarify what it means to be not just job ready, but also career ready. Here's their perspective (Career Readiness Partner Council, 2015):

> A career-ready person effectively navigates pathways that connect education and employment to achieve a fulfilling, financially secure, and successful career. A career is more than just a job. Career readiness has no defined endpoint. To be career ready in our ever-changing global economy requires adaptability and a commitment to lifelong learning, along with mastery of key knowledge, skills, and dispositions that vary from one career to another and change over time as a person progresses along a developmental continuum. Knowledge, skills, and dispositions that are inter-dependent and mutually reinforcing. These include academic and technical knowledge and skills and employability knowledge, skills and dispositions.

Have our schools responded? Yes! But are our efforts paying off? We've added more tests, requirements, regulations, and rules while continuing to prepare students for a world that no longer exists. We've doubled down on the past rather than focusing on the future.

We are no longer sending our students off to yesterday's large corporations where they would steadily climb the ranks for the duration of a career, with guaranteed benefits awaiting them at retirement. So can we, in good conscience, continue to use yesterday's model to educate our children?

How, then, do we elevate career ready to the level of college ready systemwide? How do we give both equal weight in our classrooms?

How do we teach our students to build cohesive, strong, viable, valued career portfolios? How can we prepare them to thrive and contribute productively in the twenty-first-century economy?

Put a Stake In the Ground Three to Five Years Out

Getting our students career ready, as you'll see in the ensuing chapters, is as much about technical skills as it is about softer, noncognitive skills. It's up to us to anticipate those skills, technical or otherwise, that will be valued in the future. I believe that being future-focused is a matter of mindset. Is yours a growth mindset or a fixed mindset?

Today's educators are products of the American education system. We liked school when we were kids. We went on to college to major in "school" and in our favorite subject, so when we graduated we could return to school—and do to others what had been done to us!

That's logical, I suppose. But it's also fixed in the past. Teachers: ask yourselves if you're instructing as you were instructed as a student. If the answer is yes, you know your mindset.

Being honest is half the battle—perhaps the most important part of the battle. I commend your courage if you can admit your mindset is more fixed than not.

Now choose to adopt a growth mindset. If you don't, you will continue to prepare your students for a bygone era. If you and your colleagues don't, together you will maintain and protect an educational system controlled by rules, regulations, certifications, terms, and formal legal agreements. The result is an immovable system, fixed in the past, right along with your collective mindset.

How can we develop a growth mindset?

Put a stake in the ground three to five years out. Then devise a system focused on what students must know, do, and be like over that period to succeed in this ever-more technological, information-based, rapidly changing, and not totally predictable society.

Simple to spell out; much more difficult to implement. But it's the only way to break up a mindset that keeps educators anchored in the past. Futurist author Tyler Cowen refers to it as "creative destruction":

the only way to progress is to diminish and put aside the current (Cowen, 2004).

Those who focus on career readiness are moving toward a growth mindset.

Chapter Four

Core Value 3: The Focus of Instruction Must Be Learning

What Is the Purpose of School?

In 2015, learning software company Instructure surveyed 750 U.S.-based managers to determine what they look for when evaluating millennial job candidates. As reported by Instructure vice president Jeff Weber, "When we asked managers what factors are most important to career success—not simply what they look for in hiring—managers rank industry knowledge and technical skill on par with core attributes. This suggests that in order to succeed at work, employers want millennials who can demonstrate a well-rounded capacity and interest in continual learning because the skills they need to do their job now may be vastly different than the ones they need in five to ten years" (Weber, 2015).

Ah, managers want lifelong learning! Why? Because the survey also showed that they want to hire employees "who can adapt to rapid change, solve problems on the fly, and be teachable at every phase of their career" (Weber, 2015). And because managers understand that technology changes the skills required for a job every few years.

We know that the purpose of school is to prepare students for successful careers and lives. And now we well know *why*. So what does this mean the purpose of instruction is? Logically, it should follow that the purpose of instruction should be to help students gain the skills they will need to be successful in careers and life.

And employers want lifelong learners. Because lifelong learners will learn—again and again—what they need to know to do a job well as the dynamics and forces around them change.

There's one problem: the system is arranged to keep the purpose of school and instruction focused on little more than advancing students to the next grade level. We are credentialed and contracted to keep all of our focus on getting students to achieve the milestones that will allow them to enter the next grade.

I see this again and again when I speak to educators. When I ask educators the purpose of school, the dialogue always goes like we're reading lines from a movie script:

> **Me:** Let me see a show of hands. How many third-grade teachers are out there? *(Third-grade teachers raise their hands.)* Now what's the main job of a third-grade teacher?

> **Teachers:** To get kids ready for fourth grade!

> **Me:** And what's the main job of the fourth grade teacher?

> **Teachers:** To get kids ready for fifth grade!

On and on we go, until we come to this:

> **Me:** "And what's the purpose of senior year in high school?"

> **Teachers:** "To get kids ready for college or work!"

I believe that we all know that no matter our role in education, no matter the age of the students we work with, our purpose is to prepare them for successful careers and lives. I also believe that we have been living for so long under the blanket of credentials and contracts, that we are forced to take our eyes off the ball. We are distracted by standardized tests, evaluations, and contract requirements. Before we know it, we're so focused on these other demands that we've lost sight of the long-term goals, dreams, and hopes we have for each of our students.

The result? The purpose of school becomes school itself. School has become an end in itself, not a means to an end.

Might the Fog of the Standardized Test Be Lifting?

Speaking of those onerous standardized tests, let's take a moment to examine testing—a trend that has been public education's key response to our changing world. Quite simply, standardized testing has overwhelmed teachers and students.

A 2015 study conducted by the Council of the Great City Schools, a group focused on the country's urban school districts, found that a typical student takes 112 mandated standardized tests between pre-kindergarten classes and twelfth grade. The heaviest load falls on eighth-graders, who spend an average of 25.3 hours during the school year taking standardized tests. Testing impacts even the youngest students, with the average pre-K class giving 4.1 standardized tests, the study found.

Thankfully, I believe this burdensome trend has started to decline.

In 2015, President Obama pledged to take steps to reduce testing overload, as did then-U.S. Secretary of Education Arne Duncan. Even more significantly, the federal Every Student Succeeds Act (ESSA)— the replacement to the No Child Left Behind Act—calls for a change in course. The new law still requires testing, but it turns some control back to the states and local districts to set targets for total time spent on testing. The law also eliminates redundant or unnecessary tests.

At the same time, several districts around the country have said, "Enough!" California eliminated its high school graduation test in the fall of 2015, joining Minnesota, Mississippi, Alaska, Rhode Island, and South Carolina. Miami-Dade County Public Schools, the fourth-largest district in the country, cut the number of district-created, end-of-course exams from 300 to 10.

Maybe, just maybe, we've turned a corner so we can now focus on more meaningful assessments.

The Purpose of Instruction Is Learning

It bears repeating, lest we lose sight of it again: the purpose of school is to prepare students for successful careers and lives. This means that the purpose and focus of instruction must be learning—and must be integral to vision. This holds two purposes.

First, planning only to the point of instruction only ensures that we teachers instruct. Planning to the point of learning ensures that students *learn*. When we think of instruction as ultimately about learning, then students remain at the center of our instructional planning and decisions. Where instruction puts the focus on us doing the instructing, *learning* reminds us that education is about the students, not us.

Second, in keeping the focus on learning, we will more likely make lifelong learners of all those students whom we have the pleasure of teaching. That is the foundation to being career ready in the twenty-first century. As the Instructure survey showed, employers recognize that the skills an employee needs even in the duration of his or her job could change. Thus, what matters more is a desire, an ability, and a know-how to learn, and to learn again and again over the course of an entire career.

Taking a Stand

How do we come out from under the blanket of contracts and credentials? Like those schools boldly saying "enough," so too must we. Fortunately, ESSA gives us runway to take back some control and make localized decisions. I urge you not to squander this opportunity.

The system, parents, community, and the media are still telling us to prepare students for the next grade, the next level of education. It's up to us to re-educate all our constituencies about what the true purpose of school and instruction are. Have conversations with your students' parents and your local community to explain your vision for students. Appoint people to speak to the media about why you are eschewing outdated credentials and contracts. Explain that bold measures are being taken to put the student back at the center of all decisions made.

And explain why. Remember what I said earlier: for any change initiative to work, people must first understand why the changes are being made. Educate yourselves about the economic circumstances I outline in this book. Know them well enough to be able to explain them to those whom you need to convince of your plans. Make it personal by reminding them that your ultimate goal is to make their sons or daughters or young community members as prepared as possible to grow into productive, self-sufficient citizens who can afford to put more into the system than they take out.

Data Is Your Friend: Measure What Matters

How can you tell if your students are really, truly learning? Data. How can you convince skeptical constituents and stakeholders that your plans to put students back at the center of instruction—no matter how much they appear to buck current credential- and contract-obsessed convention—are working? Data.

But only if you measure what matters.

It's not enough just to collect data. Nor is it enough to collect any data. With technology handing us so many possible data tools these days, we have to be smart and strategic about those we choose to use.

When designing your plans to make instruction about learning, talk through the milestones and indicators that will reveal if a student is or is not learning. Then track that relevant data and only that data. Determine a plan to adopt the right tools to help you analyze only relevant data in such a way that it will be actionable. If you can't take action with data, what's the point? I often say that today we are data rich, but analysis poor. Data, data everywhere, but not a drop to help us think.

In Chapter Ten, I will explain DSEI, or the Daggett System for Effective Instruction, which you may recall is a comprehensive framework to put into place successful changes, from the district to the classroom, for rigorous, relevant, career- and college-ready learning. Part of DSEI is a model for implementing a strategic, systemwide approach to tracking relevant data and using it to support student-centered decision-making. For our purposes here, keep in mind that data can be a boon when trying to win the support of constituents as you set out to implement bold initiatives to put learning at the center of instruction.

But only if you measure what matters.

Chapter Five

Core Value 4: We Must Teach Our Students to *Do*

What Does It Take to *Do*?

L earning to learn is half the battle of career ready. The second half is knowing how to take action with what one has learned. We must teach students to *do*, to act with their knowledge.

When it comes to education, *doing* is a function of two things: capacity and opportunity.

Let me explain. I'll start with capacity. *Capacity* is defined as one's actual or potential ability to perform. When a person has a capacity to perform or take action, then the person will be more likely to take that action. If someone has the capacity to play a song on the piano—if the person puts time into learning the mechanics of playing piano, learning how to read sheet music, practicing, and honing this skill—then the person can and will play. If the individual does not have the capacity to play a song on the piano, then the person won't take that action.

Consider a more career-relevant example: if an engineer has learned how engineering overlaps with psychology, biology, and marketing, then that person's capacity to act expands. The engineer can then design a smartphone that is both user-friendly and easier for the marketing team to position to ideal consumers and the sales team to sell to those customers.

Now what about opportunity as the second function of doing? We all know what *opportunity* means. In our context it means access to chances to apply knowledge through action. As it relates to the classroom, educators must ask: Are we providing our students enough opportunities to use their capacity to take action? Are we giving them opportunities to practice application of learning in different, increasingly complex scenarios? (In terms of the Rigor/Relevance Framework®, asking this question during lesson planning is also a tool to check if instruction will push learning into higher levels of real-world relevance—Quadrants B and D.)

Outside of the classroom, do our students behave in ways that protect, rather than limit, their opportunities in and after school? Are we encouraging them to make decisions that will open up as many doors of opportunity as possible, rather than engaging in risky behavior that could very well shut door after door?

In terms of our students' futures beyond their school careers, are we helping them think long term about the opportunities they hope for in the future? Are we conditioning them to consider the long-term impacts of their decisions today, of how they treat people and interact with the world? Are we telling them that what they do today can close career opportunity doors tomorrow? Are we reminding them they must begin planning for and safeguarding their futures *now*?

For us educators, this is what it means to teach our students to *do*: It means empowering them with the capacity to take action with knowledge. It means encouraging them to open as many doors as possible for opportunities to take action with knowledge. And it means helping them create a habit of always viewing their behavior in and out of school in terms of opening or closing opportunity doors—today and way down the line.

What underpins both the capacity and opportunity to do? Well, how does one find the confidence, the wherewithal to take action with knowledge? And how must one behave, interact with people, and engage in the world to open as many opportunity doors as possible, while also preventing any from being closed?

We do this by incorporating the Twelve Guiding Principles into our curriculum and learning plans whenever possible. These Guiding Principles are noncognitive skills, also called interpersonal skills, social-emotional skills, or soft skills, that both empower taking productive action and ensure that a person will continue to have countless opportunities to do so over the course of a lifetime.

The Twelve Guiding Principles of Exceptional Character

Research by ICLE shows that the Twelve Guiding Principles that follow are qualities that the vast majority of every community would agree are important for children to develop. These attributes of character influence an individual's thoughts, feelings, and behavior. They serve as guides to behavior in different settings: school, home, work, and leisure. They direct personal and interpersonal behavior in any environment and in any situation, and they evolve over a person's lifespan.

The Twelve Guiding Principles of Exceptional Character are (International Center for Leadership in Education, 2007):

1. **Adaptability**: *The ability and willingness to change*; putting oneself in harmony with changed circumstances
2. **Compassion**: *Kindness*; the desire to help others in need or distress
3. **Contemplation**: *Giving serious consideration to something, reflection*; thinking things through carefully and evaluating results of actions and decisions
4. **Courage**: *Bravery*; the willingness to put beliefs into practice; the capacity to meet danger without giving way to fear
5. **Honesty**: *Truthfulness, sincerity*; never deceiving, stealing, or taking advantage of the trust extended by others
6. **Initiative**: *Eagerness to do something*; thinking and acting on one's own ideas without prompting by others
7. **Loyalty**: *Faithfulness, dependability*; being faithful to another person in the performance or duty or adhering to a contract with another person

8. **Optimism**: *Positive beliefs*; taking a hopeful view and believing that all will work out for the best
9. **Perseverance**: *Working hard at something*; trying hard and continuously in spite of obstacles and difficulties
10. **Respect**: *Regard, value, admiration, appreciation*; special esteem or consideration in which one holds another person or thing
11. **Responsibility**: *Accountability*; considering oneself answerable for something
12. **Trustworthiness**: *Reliability*, dependability; acting in a way that deserves trust and confidence from others

Schools can use this model or devise their own lists of appropriate Guiding Principles that guide good character. What matters is that you address character in your school.

While all of these principles can be used in taking action and creating opportunities in life, consider how contemplation, courage, and optimism might make it easier for one to feel confident and comfortable taking action. Consider how initiative, perseverance, and adaptability will be invaluable when people hit setbacks, as they inevitably will.

It's easy to see how respect, compassion, and honesty can guide choices that strengthen relationships, or make for the most productive, not destructive, encounters that open doors or keep them from slamming shut. And it makes sense that responsibility, loyalty, and trustworthiness can yield opportunities for yet more responsibility, and thus more opportunities to create value, earn more income, or advance in career or relationships.

When these Guiding Principles are routinely applied in people's lives, those people will be well prepared to take productive action with knowledge, which creates a virtuous cycle of confidence building, where capacity expands that much more. They will also have more opportunities—of greater breadth and frequency—that are of personal, social, and professional value.

Importantly, the earlier we learn, practice, and make a habit of these principles, the better. The later we learn them, the more likely we are to run into trouble that squashes our confidence and shuts doors of opportunity.

Guiding Principles: Keeping Kids in School and Out of Trouble

For about five years in the early 1990s, 50 kindergarten teachers from Durham, N.C.; Nashville, Tenn.; Seattle, Wash.; and Pennsylvania took part in a study to understand how kids acquire healthy social skills. Teachers were asked to score each of their students in various social behaviors and communication skills, such as "cooperates with peers without prompting," "is helpful to others," "is very good at understanding feelings," and "resolves problems on own" (Bornstein, 2015).

After the study ended, researchers from Pennsylvania State University and Duke University stayed in touch with the participating students. The relationship between these students' social competency scores and their progress in life is stunning.

The teachers' scores of those kindergarteners' social and emotional skills were all but predictive. Higher social competency scores correlated with graduating from high school, attaining higher education, and securing a well-paying job. On the flip side, lower social competency scores correlated with a higher likelihood of dropping out of school, getting arrested, abusing drugs and alcohol, and needing government assistance or public housing (Robert Wood Johnson Foundation, 2015).

"These early [social competency] abilities, especially the ability to get along with others, are the abilities that make other kids like you, and make teachers like kids," says Mark T. Greenberg, a professor of Human Development and Psychology at Penn State and co-author of the study. "And when kids feel liked, they're more likely to settle down and pay attention, and keep out of the principal's office, and reap the benefits of being in a classroom. And this builds over time; it's like a cascade. They become more bonded with peers and healthy adults and they become more bonded to school as an institution, and all those skills lead them, independent of their I.Q., to be less at risk for problems" (Bornstein, 2015).

Guiding Principles: Keeping Employees Thriving and Employers Happy

It's clear these Twelve Guiding Principles correspond with students staying in school through at least high school graduation and the likelihood of thriving throughout and after school. As the Penn State/ Duke study revealed, the principles also increase the prospect of landing higher-paying jobs. But how about once a person is in that job? How do the principles relate to excelling in careers?

"Employers want soft skills, the ability to work on a team, and to do analysis on the job site," according to a Harvard-led school- to-work project, Creating Pathways to Prosperity: A Blueprint for Action (Harvard Graduate School of Education, 2014). All students must be empowered with more than technical expertise or academic achievement to build a strong workforce and a prosperous society.

To succeed today, workers must learn to collaborate—to "play nice with others in the sandbox." The world is amazingly diverse, and technology has shrunk our world in many ways. It's likely that today's high-skilled employee will at some point work with people who have different values and different ways of communicating. It's not just getting along with your neighbors—it's getting along with your neighbors around the globe. And because so many employees now work remotely with no defined schedule, as opposed to a traditional 9-to-5 office environment, graduates will need self-discipline and the ability to solve their own work-related problems.

In other words, today's students must develop into Renaissance individuals in a technological age. They must be adaptable, be able to solve problems, and be able to collaborate effectively, as well as possess the characteristics we've discussed in this chapter—the soft skills, I might add, that most schools are not building into their culture, campuses, or classrooms.

Incorporating the Guiding Principles into Your Schools

At ICLE, we've long observed schools that successfully promote Guiding Principles—or whatever list of principles of character a school deems appropriate for its unique DNA. First and foremost, these schools value character in both students *and* adults. This means that they regularly talk about the Guiding Principles—amongst staff and with students and families. In doing so, everyone in the school feels an obligation to contribute to an environment where *all* people are to be respected and relationships are to be valued and nurtured.

As you bring this core value to life in your school, bring it out in the open. It will make everyone a stakeholder in the creation of a respectful, character-driven environment. Students then learn these Guiding Principles by observing, mirroring, and doing. After all, their main purpose is in teaching students to *do*, and to do with character. In doing these Guiding Principles, so to speak, students and educators alike will feel accountable to them—and to each other.

Schools who *do* Guiding Principles effectively have the following key attributes:

- Teachers and administrators promote a caring community.
- Schools help students develop a commitment to Guiding Principles.
- Schools foster partnerships among students and teachers.
- Parents, teachers, and administrators demonstrate a clear, sustained commitment to initiatives taken to promote character.
- Teachers and administrators integrate Guiding Principles into the curriculum and into the fabric of school life.

Get Creative, Have Fun

The first rule of making character core to your school is to make it about everyone. The second rule is to make it fun.

We have seen educators and students get really creative and original in finding ways to fold character into curriculum and the fabric of school life. Fun is a powerful way to bond. When's the last time you had fun with someone and didn't come away feeling more camaraderie with that person? So have some fun and nurture relationships while you're at it!

Character on Campus

We've worked with educators who choose a schoolwide Guiding Principle of the Month, which is broadcasted and incorporated into staff meetings, lesson plans, pep rallies, and communications with colleagues, students, and families. Students use the principle to make banners to hang in the hallways and classrooms each month. They create ribbons and award them to staff and peers they see demonstrating that principle. They use social media to share experiences witnessing that principle in use on campus or out in the world. The opportunities for doing and discussing with Guiding Principle of the Month are endless.

We've seen schools devote a section of their school paper to Guiding Principles, like "The Character Corner." Moments of good character on campus can be written about, examples from society can be reflected upon, or discussions of a principle can be had as a fixed feature of school news.

Leadership opportunities—for staff and students—are valuable chances for people to practice acting and interacting with character. Think of ways to create more leadership opportunities for those in your school, no matter how temporary or small. Make Guiding Principles a fixture of conversations about the role and what to do once one is in the role.

Community service projects have a way of incorporating multiple facets of character at once. They show students that they are more than just themselves, that they are part of a community to which they have a responsibility. Where and when possible, community service is an enriching opportunity to foster Guiding Principles *and* strengthen all relationships involved—with peers, colleagues, friends, and the community.

Character in Classrooms

In the classroom, students must come to understand the importance of Guiding Principles. I suggest that every year, teachers take the time to "teach" students the significance of each principle in terms that align to students' age. As teachers explain the principles, they should take care to explain how they matter to the individual, between individuals, in groups, and in the world. Where possible, connect character to careers, explaining how the principles impact successful collaboration, productivity, and achievement at work.

When it comes to teaching character, positive affirmation is key. Acknowledge when your students are applying a principle. Reinforce that behavior with praise so that they will be more likely to use it again, particularly in the face of a dilemma. Encourage them to acknowledge when their own friends and family members show good character as well, so that the principles remain at the top of their minds and their positive role in relationships can be fortified.

To help students understand that character, or a lack thereof, leads to certain outcomes, inquiry-based learning—such as the Socratic method—can be effective. It helps teachers frame conversations and it encourages student participation. It's also an approach that can be adapted to most any age group. When planning an inquiry-based conversation about Guiding Principles, consider the following steps:

1. **Plan the Discussion:** Prepare an academic lesson that is application-oriented and involves people and one or more Guiding Principles. Devise at least one activity for students to be included in the lesson.

2. **Use the Socratic Method:** Ask which Guiding Principle(s) pertained to the lesson. Pose high-level questions to guide students toward defining the principle and identifying why it was important to the situation. Ask students to describe how to apply the principle in this role. Nudge them to contrast it with misguided principles and consider how the consequences would have changed. Ask students to decide if they would act from the

guided or misguided principle. Emphasize the importance of contemplation.

3. **Conclude the Lesson:** Review key aspects of the discussion. Ask students how they could apply what they learned to their own lives and what goals they want to work toward in the coming days based on their insights. Assign homework that integrates guiding principles and academic material.

Another option to bring Guiding Principles into the classroom is the five-day approach:

- **Monday:** The teacher describes a principle and an example of how to apply it.
- **Tuesday:** Students give examples of how they would apply the principle in real-life predictable and unpredictable situations.
- **Wednesday:** The teacher provides scenarios from a specific role being emphasized (e.g., parent, friend, pet owner, employee) and asks questions that will help stimulate a more rigorous understanding of that principle.
- **Thursday:** The teacher gives examples from the lesson plan and helps students understand how to generalize the principle to their personal lives.
- **Friday:** The teacher offers one good example of a project, assignment, etc., that a student completed that week, or asks and answers a question posed by a parent, teacher, or student.

Creativity and fun are also encouraged when you consider how to weave the Guiding Principles into learning and doing. To practice character in collaboration, students could work together to write and act out parallel skits, one where a principle, such as honesty, is used, resulting in a certain outcome, and one where it is not, resulting in a different outcome.

Students could read a historical text and identify aspects of character involved. For example, students could read about the drafting and signing of the Declaration of Independence. You could ask students to assume the role of journalist and write an article about the Guiding

Principles they recognized in that historical moment and time and their impact on it. Ask them to consider the outcome if misguided principles had been driving key people in that moment.

Students could do mock job interviews, where each partner rates the other on indicators of Guiding Principles. They could develop a proposal for submission to the board of education to launch a student recognition program based on the Guiding Principles. They could watch and analyze commercials to look for signs of Guiding Principles, or a lack thereof, in them and then write an essay about how those ads made them feel.

Science students could reflect on the role of honesty experiments. Math students could reflect on the role of perseverance in problem solving. Physical education students and athletes could reflect on the role of trustworthiness in team sports. History students could reflect on game-changing moments of courage throughout history. Foreign language students could reflect on the role of respect between cultures. English students could reflect on the role of compassion in communication. Music students could reflect on the role of initiative in composing songs.

From there, to empower your students to take action with their knowledge, teachers could partner with teachers in other disciplines to swap principles. The physical education students could be asked to apply what they've learned about trustworthiness in team sports to conducting science experiments with partners. The foreign language students could be asked to apply what they learned about respect between cultures to analyze those game-changing moments of courage in history. And so on, and so forth. Each of these presents an opportunity for merging an academic lesson with a Guiding Principle lesson. And each presents an opportunity for students to demonstrate their capacity to *do*.

Get creative. Have fun. Be courageous. And then *do*.

Chapter Six

Core Value 5: Educators Must Think Like Entrepreneurs

Large Organizations: Surrounded by Specialists

In 1975, I joined the New York State Department of Education. Before that I taught and served as an administrator in various places: two years at Amsterdam High School in Amsterdam, N.Y.; two years at Alfred State College in Alfred, N.Y.; one year at Temple University in Philadelphia, where I also completed a doctorate in the school of education, and then at Russell Sage College in Troy, N.Y., where I directed the school of business administration for one year. At each stop, I taught courses that prepared students for the business world. Every course I taught was specialized, narrow, and focused.

Then I moved on to the New York State Department of Education. The skills I used there were the same ones I had taught—only now, I applied them to education instead of business. If I faced a personnel issue, I would talk with Human Resources. If I faced a financial problem, I would talk with someone in the Division of Finance. Communications? Travel? You get the idea.

Specialists surrounded me all day, every day.

Small Organizations: Surrounded by Generalists

It was a huge adjustment when I started the International Center for Leadership in Education. For the first time in my working career, I was on my own. I had no HR department, no finance or travel departments. From day one, I had to figure out how to do payroll and dozens of other unfamiliar tasks.

Each day I confronted new questions: How do I market? How do I sell? How do I serve the requirements of many different clients? How do I handle the ebb and flow of work? How do I keep my message fresh?

To succeed, I had to develop new skills—a lot of them. I had to transition from being a specialist—who relied on a team of other specialists—to a generalist. In the state education department, when I didn't know what to do or where to turn, I called someone. Now I had to figure it out myself.

It was a struggle, but as ICLE grew, I began to see the bigger picture. I saw where I needed to make connections, because I had performed just about every job in the company. I saw how I needed to organize the company. I began hiring generalists—more people who knew how to do lots of things.

I learned an important lesson as the years passed: efficiency helps make a company successful.

I look back at my years at the state education department and see all kinds of inefficiencies. In large organizations, simple tasks become complex because you must touch base with so many different people. In a smaller company, the leader makes a decision and moves on to the next issue.

How We Work—and the Skills Needed—Is Shifting

According to a report on business trends prepared by Intuit, the financial software company headquartered in Silicon Valley, the majority of jobs from here on out will likely be with smaller companies (Intuit, 2007). A Small Business & Entrepreneurial Council trends report echoes this prediction. Working for a large company isn't as attractive as it used to be, the report finds, because of long, often inflexible work schedules, dwindling benefits, and less job security (Small Business and Entrepreneurship Council, 2016).

"As a result, large-company employment has fallen steadily for several decades," the Intuit report says. "Today less than 40 percent of Americans work for companies with more than 1,000 employees. At the same time, small business employment continues to climb, both in absolute numbers and as a percentage of total employment."

The decline of jobs at large companies is resulting in new and more independent ways of working. Business author Daniel Pink, in his book *Free Agent Nation*, describes this shift in employment practices. Instead of working for a specific company, people increasingly are developing skills they can take from job to job. At the same time, companies are looking for more flexible work arrangements from their employees. This combination has resulted in more "free-agent" contract relationships that meet the needs of both workers and employers (Pink, 2002).

Intuit estimates there are 7 million contract-oriented small businesses in the country. Does this matter?

It does, and here's why: the workplace of a large company is far different from the workplace of a small or contract-driven company. The skills you need in each are fundamentally different. The skills you need to navigate a career through large companies (career path) and among several smaller companies (career portfolio) are fundamentally different.

At large companies, workers tend to need area expertise or specialization, as large corporations are structured entirely around areas of expertise. People work in specific departments organized by skill. Marketers work in the marketing department. Salespeople work in the sales department. Operations people work in the operations department. Finance people work in the finance department. The chain of command is clear. In fact, it's often set in stone in nifty, corporate hierarchy charts, such as the following example.

Corporate Hierarchy Structure

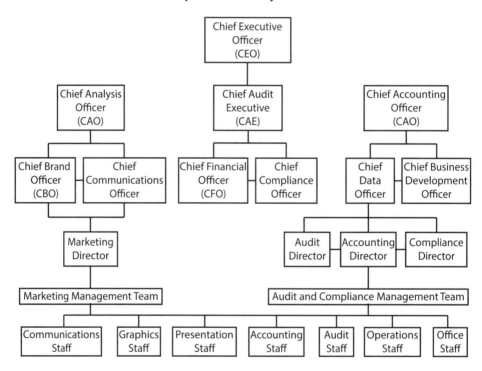

With the neatly organized structures of large firms, there's usually known protocol (read: bureaucracy) for communicating up or attempting to make decisions in the chain of command. Systems and structures are typically well defined, and often have been for years. There is clarity in this, but there is also a lack of flexibility—in processes and roles. People who thrive in large corporations are those who like to work within established systems, are risk averse, take direction well, and prefer to operate under little to no ambiguity.

Life is totally different at smaller and entrepreneurial companies. The advantage that comes with smaller firms is flexibility. Employees at these companies can react quickly to changing market dynamics, technologies, customer preferences, or economic circumstances. When there are fewer people at a firm, there's less bureaucracy around decision-making and taking action. People are expected to take initiative. If there are systems and structures, they tend to be more flexible, and there is often more openness to evolving them if they become outdated.

At these more agile companies, there tends not to be a rigid hierarchy, but rather teams of people with broader knowledge and skillsets and more agency. The organizational chart tends to be flatter, with more distributed leadership and areas of overlap between teams or departments. This often means more transparency and employees are more likely to be aware of what's going on over on that other team or in that other section of the office.

Frequent collaboration is facilitated—and expected—when an employee has a basic knowledge of what others on the team are doing. These people, with a broad knowledge base across many areas and a deep expertise in one area, are often called "T-shaped" people. They are the types of people who will be the most well-equipped and prepared for successful careers in smaller, more entrepreneurial companies. Imagine how much more swiftly decisions can be made when people have flatter learning curves about other facets of the company and their industry at large.

However, in small companies, problems sometimes arise because employees frequently have to "do it all." Often it's not "responsibilities as assigned" as much as "responsibilities as needed." This creates ambiguity, and those who excel in these circumstances are those who can tolerate uncertainty and are drawn to taking initiative and responsibility for decision-making amid murkiness.

Our economy is pushing more and more workers away from large corporations and into entrepreneurial environments. What does this mean for educators? At this point, I trust you know the answer.

Something Is Wrong with This Picture

Let's take a look at the typical district and school organizational chart.

School District Organization Chart

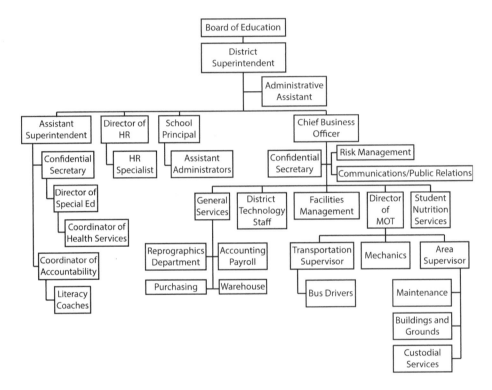

Look familiar? Our districts and schools are structured just like large corporations.

Consider your role in your school or district. Is it narrow in focus? Based on area expertise? Hemmed in by rigid expectations and procedures? Likely yes.

What about decision-making and action taking? Is how decisions are made clearly defined and stringent? Are there tight protocols around process before taking action? Likely yes.

Consider how you organize the information you teach. Are your students, particularly as they advance in grades, placed in "subject silos"? Likely yes.

Just as layers of rules, regulations, contracts, and other requirements dictate the behavior of large corporations and their employees, rules, regulations, certifications, tenure, and standardized policies rule school positions and processes.

This is even more pronounced on college and university campuses. Higher education is organized into even more specialized courses and in-depth concentrations and majors. Professors work in narrow areas of specialization—and as a former professor I can say that with confidence! They work in their own silos and, as a result, not all professors can help students see the connections between and across disciplines.

As long as our districts and schools remain rigidly set up like large corporations, then our high school and college students will continue to graduate with more in-depth knowledge in a specialized area—exactly what large corporations have traditionally wanted and needed.

Reorganizing and Rethinking for the Entrepreneurial Economy

We are out of excuses. We educators have to change how we teach our students and how our students learn if we are going to give them the best chances for success in our technology-driven, globalized, increasingly entrepreneurial economy. We have to change if we are going to maintain the historical strength of our economy, which has brought prosperity to more of its citizens than any other nation in history. We have to change if we want to continue to provide benefits and support to our fellow citizens in need. And we have to change if we hope to fund both equity and excellence in public education so every last child in our country can be the hope of our future.

We as individual educators and as an education industry have to change. That we have created and tolerated a situation where it is nearly impossible to change merely the bell or bus schedule can no longer be okay. It is these sorts of things that we have always accepted to go along to get along to which we must begin to say, "No!" Decide that accepting these systems as "facts" is no longer part of your culture, vision, or mindset as a twenty-first-century educator. Decide that business as usual is no longer going to be your business as usual.

We as individuals must become more nimble, flexible, innovative, and capable, just like entrepreneurs. We must do this so we can be the agents of change our communities so desperately need. And we must do this so that we can begin to create more flexible and innovative classrooms, schools, and districts, ripe for total overhaul to meet the needs of today's students.

There is an added invaluable benefit to becoming more entrepreneurial educators who work in more entrepreneurial schools and districts. By doing so, we will mirror these skills to our students. They too will need these skills to survive and thrive in smaller, more entrepreneurial organizations. If we inhabit these skills ourselves, we will more naturally incorporate learning them into our curriculum, lesson plans, and extracurricular activities. We will also familiarize our students with working and learning in entrepreneurial settings— just like the ones most will very likely find themselves working in professionally one day.

The Mindset of the Successful Entrepreneur

What does it take to act and think like a successful entrepreneur? In my experience and observation, a list compiled by ActionCoach, a global business coaching firm, and summarized here, rings true. But like any good entrepreneur, you must assert your individuality, initiative, creativity, and originality and come up with a list of your own that rings true for you and your school or district.

Successful entrepreneurs (ActionCoach, 2016):

- **Are confident**: Not everyone is born with confidence, but that does not mean you are not capable of developing it.
- **Develop a sense of ownership**: An entrepreneur takes responsibility for getting things done—and does them with care and attention to detail. Rather than seeing a problem as someone else's to fix, the business owner takes it on as his or her own, and ultimately takes pride in finding a solution.

- **Communicate well:** A small-business owner recognizes that people are key. Clients, employees, and strategic partners make or break a business. Communication is essential to ensure successful relationships. Clearly written and spoken directions, and the ability to listen, are absolute musts.
- **Have a passion for learning:** Successful entrepreneurs are usually autodidactic learners; much of what they know comes from experience. They did not learn it in a classroom. They surround themselves with people who know more than they do.
- **Are team players:** Without building a team, entrepreneurs shoulder the burden themselves. One twig can be easily broken, but a bundle of twigs becomes stronger than the sum of its individual parts. Successful small businesses leverage teamwork to get the heavy lifting done without breaking stride.
- **Build systems:** Good systems allow business owners to produce great results every time. Successful entrepreneurs rely on strong systems. If an employee gets the job done but then falls sick or leaves, the job is threatened. But if the owner creates a system to get the job done, anyone can step in and follow the blueprint.
- **Are dedicated:** One of the biggest reasons companies fail is they lose focus. A successful business owner brings a single-minded dedication to the task and is committed to a positive outcome. Target a goal, clarify the objective, refine the brand, and narrow the margin of error.
- **Are grateful:** Being grateful for what we have opens us up to receive more. Entrepreneurs who are grateful appreciate what they've been given. They respect it and nurture it. Successful small business owners take nothing for granted.
- **Are optimistic:** Optimism is essential. Successful owners know setbacks are valuable lessons and learnings gained through first-hand experience. They relegate failures or disappointments to the past.
- **Are outgoing:** Business is all about people, which means successful entrepreneurs tend to be socially outgoing. They get excited about sharing ideas, products, and services, and that excitement is contagious to employees, clients, and friends.

- **Lead by example:** Successful entrepreneurs are self-starters who jump into tasks with enthusiasm, but also are skilled at leading others. They know the importance of teamwork. Perry M. Smith, business consultant and retired Air Force major general, once wrote: "Leaders who share their power and their time can accomplish extraordinary things. The best leaders understand that leadership is the liberation of talent; hence they gain power not only by constantly giving it away, but also by not grabbing it back."
- **Are fearless:** Many people could be successful if they only took chances. Instead they cling to what is familiar, even if it means not fulfilling their dreams. Successful entrepreneurs approach life so that success far outweighs the fear of failure.

How can you and your teams incorporate these attitudes and behaviors into your vision? And your conversations and decision-making processes? And the actions you take as you set out to prepare *all* of your students for the world that awaits them?

However you can, please do. Because, again, we are out of excuses.

Looking Outside to Help Us Look Within

As we as educators should habitually do, let's look at what's happening in the world outside of education. As we've discussed, industry after industry is getting the technology treatment, where a layer of technology is fundamentally changing the long-standing way business had been done for decades. To the rigid-minded, these technologies feel threatening. To the entrepreneurially minded, these technologies are an exciting opportunity to do big and transformative things.

Uber, launched in 2009, connects consumers to drivers to get from point A to point B. Via Uber's smartphone app, customers submit a trip request, which is then routed to Uber drivers, who use their own cars to pick up and deliver customers. Uber is available in almost 60 countries and more than 400 cities worldwide. In late 2015, Uber was worth $62.5 billion—yet it owns no cars, limos, or vans.

Airbnb, founded in 2008 in San Francisco, is a website where people list, find, and rent short-term vacation accommodations. It owns no hotels, motels, or apartments, yet it offers more private rooms than many of the largest global hotel groups, such as Hilton, Marriott, and InterContinental. According to a Barclay's research report, Airbnb could boast 129 million room-nights per year by the end of 2016 (Mudallal, 2015). The company represents as much as 17.2 percent of the hotel room supply in New York, 11.9 percent in Paris, and 10.4 percent in London. Those percentages will only increase. Its value? More than $25 billion (Demos, 2015).

Does anyone out there not know about Facebook? Can we all admit that Facebook has changed society in profound ways? As a teenage student at Harvard, Mark Zuckerberg started Facebook in his dorm room in 2004. Its growth has been phenomenal: in 2004, one million of us "liked" it. Today, Facebook has more than 1.65 billion monthly active users worldwide.

The genius of Facebook is that it allows people to connect over long distances and reconnect over lost years. "The important takeaway from Facebook's rise is that people have a desire to connect broadly," says Danah Boyd, Microsoft principal researcher and author of the book, *It's Complicated: The Social Lives of Networked Teens*. "For the longest time, technology limited communication to one on one; just think of the telephone. But now our worlds are complicated networks that overlap. The implications of that have yet to be fully realized" (Della Cava, 2014).

Alibaba is the largest e-commerce company in the world—and a company you've probably never heard of. Larger than Amazon and eBay combined, the China-based company provides consumer-to-consumer, business-to-consumer, and business-to-business sales service through web portals. Dominating 80 percent of China's online shopping market, Alibaba's transactions across its sites totaled $248 billion last year alone (LaJoie & Shearman, 2015).

"Most companies, when they're doing good, they enjoy today's wonderful life," says Jack Ma, Alibaba's founder and executive chairman. "They don't worry about five years later—but I worry about five years later" (LaJoie & Shearman, 2015).

Put a stake in the ground five years out and anticipate what the market—or students—will need. Build a business plan—or a lesson plan—from there.

Each of these companies has achieved enormous, groundbreaking success. Change was not a threat, but an opportunity. They bucked business as usual. They made future-focused decisions. And they looked fearlessly, confidently, and boldly outside the box—outside the status quo—for creative, game-changing ideas and solutions.

A Final Thought

Last winter, I was scheduled on an early evening flight to deliver a keynote presentation the next morning. Bad weather forced the airline to cancel my flight. What to do? I simply rebooked on another airline and paid for the ticket myself.

Back in my state education department days, I would have had to contact the travel department to reschedule my flight. Just one problem: the department is only open from 9 a.m. to 5 p.m. The department would have been closed, and I would have missed the event, panicked the event organizers, and missed the opportunity to meet and work with its attendees.

Innovation. Risk-reward. Flexibility. Nimbleness. That's the future. That's the new normal. Has your school caught up?

Chapter Seven

Core Value 6: Districts and Schools Must Adopt Zero-Based Budgeting

By Now You Know

By now, you see that our students are the hope of the future—theirs, ours, and our nation's. And you appreciate why. By now, you realize that career ready can no longer be second to college ready, but instead must be equal. Because not every student needs to go to college, nor can afford to take on the crushing debt college so often comes with today. And because to fail to prepare *all* our students for twenty-first-century careers is to fail to do our jobs as educators.

By now, you understand that ultimately we must teach our students to learn. You know that employers want and will reward lifelong learners who've developed a love of learning and the ability to both remain teachable and learn on their own.

By now, you accept that we must nurture students' capacity to take action with their knowledge. You're aware that you must steer them toward keeping as many opportunity doors open and learning how to open their own. You understand that the Guiding Principles underpin productive *doing*.

By now, you grasp how essential an entrepreneurial mindset is in your approach to district and school organization, decision-making, and action taking. You see how an entrepreneurial mindset will liberate you and your colleagues from the decaying, outdated systems and structures that are keeping you stuck in the past. And you recognize that in acting like an entrepreneur in your work, you will mirror the entrepreneurial attitudes and behaviors that your students will need to navigate successful careers and lives.

By now, you know that you—we—are out of excuses.

Now what? Now you and your colleagues must figure out how to, one by one, clear anything and everything obstructing your ability to bring to life a vision that *makes your school work* for today's students.

Breaking Down the Budget Roadblock

Again and again, I see the same large roadblock on the path to making schools work in the twenty-first century: the budget.

More accurately, it is the mindset behind the budget that creates the roadblock. And that mindset is the belief that the budget is more or less fixed every year. Budgeting based on last year stymies innovation and real change in two ways: financially and psychologically.

In most districts and schools, as we plan the budget for the next year, we start with last year's budget. We look at our present classrooms, teachers, and instructional programs, and this becomes our point of departure. Then we ask what it will cost to keep the budget in place. Typically, it costs about three or four percent more. We expect a hike of a percentage point or two for general inflation, and another percentage point or two for contracts.

Where will we find the money to fund these cost increases? We can't cut contract expenses, so we have to look to "non-essential" expenses. Unfortunately, this often means we chip away at supposedly less critical expenses, like professional development and travel for it, that are in fact among the most critical expenses, in my view.

There. Budget done. Now let's put the same plans as last year into place.

We go into budgeting thinking that the best way to budget is to work with what's in place. We are conditioned to believe budgets are more or less set in stone. So we move this around, and move that around. The budget becomes akin to a checkers game, rather than one of its greatest potentials: a resource to enable and fund innovation and growth. If we think the budget must stay more or less intact, we will never find the resources for innovation.

When we start with last year's budget (which is really the budget of the year before that, and the year before that, and the year before that, and on and on), we are psychologically and financially prevented from being innovation-minded. Instead, we are budgeting from a fixed mindset. We do little more than build our future based on our past.

Zero-Based Budgeting: The Ultimate Growth Mindset Budget

By definition, the zero-based budgeting approach to financial planning liberates any organization from its past. And it does this year after year. Each year brings a reset, an opportunity to set goals and budget and plan from there. For some time, the most future-focused and leading edge businesses in the private sector have been adopting zero-based budgeting as a vehicle for efficiency and innovation.

Investopedia defines zero-based budgeting as "a method of budgeting in which all expenses must be justified for each new period. Zero-based budgeting starts from a 'zero base,' and every function within an organization is analyzed for its needs and costs. Budgets are then built around what is needed for the upcoming period, regardless of whether the budget is higher or lower than the previous one" (Investopedia, 2016).

Imagine that! Imagine if every financial period, you and your colleagues had to defend each expense. Pause for just a moment. How many of your expenses would you want to fight for? How many would you happily toss aside? Probably a significant number of them.

Zero-based budgeting builds logic and a future focus into the planning process. It ensures that all expenses are relevant and are investments in the future, not mere legacy costs held over from yesteryear and investments in the past. This thinking drives efficiency, as it forces organizations to cut expenses that no longer serve their *current* goals. Sound familiar? Efficiency is the advantage of nimble, entrepreneurial companies that can react to real-time circumstances and changing needs.

Yet the real power of zero-based budgeting is in how it routinely relies on conversations about big goals and the innovative steps, systems, structures, and staffing necessary to achieve them. The process itself encourages continual goal- and innovation-oriented thinking.

Just imagine if instead of beginning to build your budget by asking, "What will it cost to keep last year's budget in place?" you asked "What do we need to do and change *right now* to prepare every student in our school for successful careers and lives?"

In terms of the Rigor/Relevance Framework® detailed in Chapter Nine, beginning with last year's budget will all but guarantee that next year's plans will not and cannot move beyond Quads A/C. We are regulated, certified, tenured, and contracted around Quads A/C—specific knowledge and expertise. So we direct all of our financial resources to those priorities and repeatedly find we have no room left to fund Quads B/D innovations and initiatives.

This may have worked fine back when preparing students for college was little different from preparing them for careers. This may have worked fine back when we funneled students into large, siloed corporations where specialized knowledge was the key to success. But Internet technologies changed that all. Today, our students need Quads B/D skills to survive and thrive in our interdisciplinary, unpredictable, Quads B/D world.

To prove that a fixed mindset approach to budgeting and planning traps educators in Quads A/C, I share an unsettling story.

Back in 1985, when I was a director in the New York Education Department, I co-authored a textbook. It was called *Technology for Tomorrow*, published by South-Western Publishing Co.

I'm embarrassed to admit this, but what I'm about to tell you illustrates a sad truth.

Today, in 2016, I still receive royalties from sales of that book. Somewhere in this country, teachers and school districts are ordering *Technology for Tomorrow* and are teaching it in their classrooms, despite the fact that it was written more than a decade before Google was created and more than two decades before the iPhone was created—really!

I'd like to think that the words I wrote were timeless, but I know better. Flipping through the pages of the book today is like looking at an ancient manuscript. Knowing that my textbook is still being used somewhere is truly scary and shocking. Why some districts believe the content is still relevant is incomprehensible, not to mention downright unfair to students.

If this doesn't convince you of just how many educators budget and plan on autopilot, I don't know what will.

How to Implement Change—Realistically

I'm sure you're thinking, "How could it be possible to up and adopt an entirely new approach to budgeting?" And you are right to ask. We are all dismayed at how futile it can be to try to change the bell schedule. How could we expect to ever overhaul the budgeting process?

I don't expect this. At least not at once and not straight away. I understand that district and school budgets and educational programming are hemmed in by contracts, policies, and laws. I understand that credentials requirements put real limits on who can teach what, when, where, and how.

So, I encourage you to experiment where you can. As I have been known to say, change must be evolutionary, not revolutionary. Revolutionaries get killed. Evolutionary change tends to be more comfortable and less threatening to most, and therefore more likely to succeed. Experiment where there's room and with those who have an appetite for it. Be patient, but deliberate. Take baby steps and calculated risks. Just start *somewhere*.

This attitude of just starting somewhere is a hallmark of the nation's most rapidly improving schools. The more innovative schools we've worked with throughout the years have figured out how and where they can break the rules. They understand when the old system isn't working, so they blow up the parts of it they can and start experimenting with what does work. But they don't do it overnight, and they don't change everything at once. What sets these schools apart is that they start with the manageable goal of getting unstuck. All this has to mean is taking some sort of action, no matter how small, with their knowledge that they must change.

Sit down with key members of your team and commit to asking again and again where there is some wiggle room for experimentation. Don't give up until you've pinpointed at least a few areas in the budget where you can toss out the old norms and toss in some big goals and then budget and tweak systems and structures to achieve them.

From there, I suggest starting with the top one third of educators who have the desire and disposition for rolling up their sleeves, tackling big challenges, implementing real changes, and assuming leadership along the way. You know this one-third by their enthusiasm for always trying out the latest promising concept and for their creativity and fearlessness.

What typically happens is that once this top third has smoothly transitioned into a new and effective way of doing things, the middle third, the cautious "wait and see" crowd, will warm to the changes and join in. This group is curious, and they are usually comfortable trying out new ideas once they've proven viable.

Then there is the final third. They are...stubborn. They have their ways of doing things, so they prefer that you take your change elsewhere, thank you very much. That said, most will give in to change if they find themselves in the conspicuous minority not yet on board. Or they'll move on. Slow, steady, subtle pressure is usually the winning strategy for this crew.

Districts of Innovation

For inspiration in chipping away at the old system and replacing it with one designed around innovation, look into Districts of Innovation in Texas. Passed by Texas' Congress in Spring 2015, Districts of Innovation provides Texas public school districts the opportunity to apply for Districts of Innovation designation.

Selected districts are eligible for exemption from a number of state statutes. What this means in practical terms is that districts:

- gain greater control in determining the educational and instructional models appropriate for their students;
- are given certain freedoms and increased flexibility, still with accountability, relative to state mandates that dictate educational programming;
- are given the tremendous gift of thinking and acting creatively, openly, differently, and outside the rigidness of certain standards, contracts, and credentials (Spring Branch ISD, 2015).

In liberation, albeit admittedly still with some defined limits, participating schools are free to make decisions that will more efficiently and effectively help them serve their students. To this end, here's an example I love from one of the Districts of Innovation schools.

Jason Massey teaches automotive technology at Dripping Springs High School. His qualifications? Credentialed he is not. Experienced he is. Massey has worked in the automotive field for 15 years. He even owns his own business designing and building race cars (Taboada, 2016). His students are, in my opinion, very lucky. They are apt to get an interdisciplinary, relevant view of automotive technologies, one that could span to include business skills, customer insights, or real-world market and industry challenges and opportunities. Not to mention a current view. Massey's experience means he knows how technologies are changing what people need to be successful in the automotive industry today and down the line. How's that for career ready instruction?

Massey does not hold the state teaching certificate otherwise required to teach a specific subject in Texas. But thanks to Districts of Innovation and the bold leaders behind the decision to hire Massey, a person who couldn't be more qualified to teach an automotive technology class has not been barred from sharing his wealth of knowledge and knowhow with students.

Use ESSA to Your Advantage

Not every state has a Districts of Innovation-like program. And this is where our confident, fearless, open-minded, nimble, new entrepreneurial mindset will come in handy. Entrepreneurs are undaunted by what is not available. Instead, they will ask how they can get started with what is.

What is available to you is the federal Every Student Succeeds Act (ESSA). Although not without its faults, I'm sure, ESSA is a landmark in one key way: it is giving more control back to states and local districts to determine how educators will monitor and evaluate student learning and progress. ESSA has blown the door wide open for candid conversations with local school boards, colleagues, and communities to create the most appropriate indicators of achievement for your students, your school, your district.

Of course, ESSA is not a carte blanche invitation to overhaul your school or district. But remember what the most successful entrepreneurs do—they seize or create opportunity where others don't yet see it. Consider ESSA an opening to begin experimenting with that top one third. Keep in mind what the nation's most rapidly improving schools do—they begin somewhere. Take at least one step, no matter how small, to get unstuck.

Just start *somewhere*.

Part Two

Frameworks and Resources to Execute Change with Success

From decades of observing both schools that have successfully implemented broad changes and schools that have failed in their attempts to do so, I know this to be true: change is best delivered thoughtfully, systematically, and methodically. A haphazard approach will guarantee failure and disillusionment.

To that end, in this section, we provide resources and frameworks to organize your thinking, planning, and execution of the big changes we know we must make.

Chapter Eight lists ICLE's current emerging trends and employment-skills research. We at ICLE have made a habit of keeping tabs both on developments we see inside education and well beyond that will transform or require transformation in how we teach. We also routinely monitor employment data, as the contraction and expansion of industries and jobs informs the skills that should be taught in our classrooms. As the education industry, the economy, technologies, and employment data shift, so too do our observations and insights about them. Check back regularly at www.leadered.com for our latest thinking in these areas.

In Chapter Nine, the Rigor/Relevance Framework® is introduced in detail. The Framework is a tool I created with ICLE colleagues more than 25 years ago to guide educators as they plan and evaluate curriculum, instruction, and assessment—and it is as relevant today as it was two decades ago. Its purpose is to make certain that learning is moving from knowledge acquisition to knowledge application. In other words, it is a methodical check for both college- and career-ready instruction and learning.

Finally, the Daggett System for Effective Instruction (DSEI) is explained in Chapter Ten. The DSEI is a district-to-classroom framework to organize, plan, and execute systemic change *with success*. Through the DSEI, all people in and components of a district are considered, respected, and strategically aligned to important transformations we owe it to our students to make.

Chapter Eight

Planning Today for Tomorrow

Culture Trumps Strategy. Vision Drives Decisions.

Where to begin? That is the question. Without a culture that can support change, no change will ever be realized. Before you take that first step, no matter how small, to getting unstuck, take a look at your culture. Is it friendly to change, strategic improvements, and innovation? Or will any attempts to renovate systems and structures be met with hostility, frustration, or resistance?

If you don't have a culture to support change, don't yet bother with that small step. Begin first by figuring out how to change your culture. Have conversations with your colleagues and peers. Understand what it is about your culture that makes change feel so unwelcome or threatening. Listen closely and hear your people's or colleagues' concerns and fears. Take them seriously and address them as you set out to transform your culture into one of empowerment and distributed leadership, where change can manifest with and through your people.

Next, sit down with key members of your team. Ask guiding questions that will get at your school's or district's core values. Use this book and the proven core values of rapidly improving schools to structure your conversations. Adapt the wisdom of these schools to fit your school's DNA. Develop other core values you deem critical in your quest to prepare *all* students for successful lives and careers in the twenty-first century. And then vet all plans, decisions, and initiatives against your vision, rejecting those that do not advance or protect it. *Vision drives decisions*.

Then, begin somewhere.

The Future Is a Good Place to Start

We are aiming to remodel our districts and schools into environments rich with the insights and resources purposefully selected to prepare students for life and careers in the world awaiting them. So, the future is usually a good place to start thinking about what those insights and resources need to be.

I know you don't have a crystal ball. Yet I also know we must be future focused when we plan instruction and learning. This means putting a stake in the ground three to five years out, imagining what skills will be in demand in the working world then, and tracking backward to incorporate learning those skills into your classrooms today.

At ICLE, we are constantly keeping an eye out for emerging trends happening around us that will impact what students need to learn today for success tomorrow. We refresh and share these trends regularly as a resource for educators. And we encourage all educators to develop a habit of completing this exercise with their teams every year.

In this chapter, we will share our latest thinking on the trends inside and outside of education that can drive your instructional choices and plans toward twenty-first-century relevance. Please discuss these insights with your colleagues and use them to help you get unstuck and well on your way to real, future-focused change.

Begin with the end—or in this case, the probable future—in mind.

Five Emerging Trends

As of the printing of this book in 2016, we at ICLE see the following five trends as critical considerations for all educators making budgetary, organizational, curricular, instructional, and learning plans.

Emerging Trend #1: Understanding, Responding to, and Preparing for More Technology in the Workplace

Technology certainly has impacted our personal lives. Just ask Siri or Cortana. It's amazing what the ubiquitous smartphone can do these days. The combination of portability, instant accessibility, and utility means it has replaced a number of devices.

A survey conducted by Prosper Business Development, an Ohio company that tracks how people use their smartphones, revealed that smartphones have replaced the following devices at the corresponding rates (Wissinger, 2011):

- Alarm clock: 61.1 percent
- GPS: 52.3 percent
- Digital camera: 44.3 percent
- Personal planner: 41.6 percent
- Landline telephone: 40.3 percent
- MP3 player: 37.6 percent
- Video camera: 34.2 percent
- Newspaper: 28.2 percent
- Radio: 27.5 percent
- Desktop/laptop computer: 24. 2 percent
- Gaming device: 20.8 percent
- Books: 20.1 percent
- Internet service at home: 19.5 percent
- DVD player: 14.1 percent

If you wound the clock back 15 years, what would you see? People holding phones up to their ears instead of people staring at phones in their hands. People gathered around a television to watch the news, a movie, or a show. People arranging themselves for a photograph, while the photographer holds a camera that was only meant to be a camera.

We take our smartphones for granted, but we must remember that smartphone technology has impacted virtually every sector of society—except one.

That's right: schools.

Educators in most schools don't allow students to use their smartphones. Why? They'll cheat, of course! Yet, aren't smartphones the very example of the technology students will be asked to use once they leave school? (And, as you probably know, these digital natives already rightly use their smartphones to locate information everywhere except, maybe, in school.)

Do you believe technology has reached its peak? Of course not. Its influence is increasing at an ever-accelerating rate. Our kids will face a world we can't fully comprehend.

Let's look at other examples of accelerating technology.

The Fusion is Ford Motor Company's low-end economy car, but it's getting some high-tech features. Ford has embedded wireless sensors in the Fusion's front bumper. As noted earlier, today's cars contain hundreds of sensors, each one generating more computing power than a 1990 mainframe computer. The Fusion's sensors can identify a pothole in the road ahead, calculate its length, depth, and width, and then communicate with the Fusion's dynamic shock absorbers, which are able to lift the car just enough to avoid the pothole. No pothole, no damage. Incredible!

Automotive technology is the second largest career and technical education (CTE) program in the country. Auto tech classrooms typically take up huge spaces to accommodate the related tools, machines, work stations, and apparatus, not to mention parking spaces for the vehicles being used for hands-on training. Many students take or have taken auto tech courses, either out of personal interest or as an entry-level pathway to a potentially well-paying career. In the past, that was probably a wise choice for many: U.S. auto repair businesses currently employ about 531,000 mechanics and generate $58 billion in revenue (IBISWorld, 2016).

Today, however, auto technology is morphing from an intervention industry to a prevention industry. It's moving from vehicles needing repairs to vehicles that have the "smart" capacity to avoid needing many repairs. The implications are staggering. There could be a dramatic reduction in the number of auto mechanics in the next five years—perhaps by as much as 80 percent—according to many auto executives.

Today's auto mechanics must become tomorrow's auto technicians. But unfortunately, many auto tech educators don't have the facilities, technologies, current expertise, curriculum, or methodology to address the issue.

We see similar shifts in other fields. The medical field is also moving from an intervention model to a prevention model. Doctors and other healthcare providers—"encouraged" by cost conscious healthcare insurers—will be increasingly measured by how many ailments they have prevented, not merely "treated." How will this impact a doctor's approach to each patient's care? One could imagine a heightened need for interpersonal skills, as prevention requires more conversations with each patient about making healthier lifestyle choices.

"Robo-financial advisors" will manage your investments. The increasingly popular hybrid robo/personal model, where substantial software is added to human interaction, is expected to account for 10 percent of all investable assets by 2025 (My Private Banking, 2016). What do you want your investments to accomplish and by when? Technology will analyze more data, including predictive data, and will do it faster and more accurately than any team of certified financial planners or investment consultants. That is also why there will be a 94 percent decrease in the number of accountants and auditors we need (Frey & Osborne, 2013).

Recall that if an algorithm can be written for a job, the person doing that job will either be looking for work or managing greater volumes of work with fewer human colleagues. Workforce research company and consultancy McKinsey & Co. reports that already existing technologies could eliminate 45 percent of the work activities in all jobs in the next three to five years (Chui, Manyika, & Miremadi, 2015). In early 2016, there were 5.6 million job openings in the United States. When we run those numbers, we cannot deny the implications on employment opportunities.

Americans are taking notice. A 2016 survey by the Pew Research Center found that 65 percent of adults expect that by 2026, robots and computers will "definitely" or "probably" do much of the work currently being done by humans (Hahn, 2016).

What's the takeaway? Are schools preparing students for jobs that won't exist in the near future?

Emerging Trend #2: A Demographic Shift

The U.S. population is aging. The number of Americans receiving disability payments has risen, and many baby boomers are reaching retirement age. Teenagers and young adults are working less and spending more time in school, supposedly to improve their chances for employment. Female workforce participation remains below male participation, and male participation has been declining since the late 1940s (Leubsdorf, 2016).

What does *The Wall Street Journal* conclude? "Lower participation and slower growth in the labor force will constrain the U.S. economy's capacity to expand, barring a pickup in productivity growth. That could limit gains in living standards, the government's ability to pay its bills, and the economy's staying power in the face of unexpected shocks."

"It's not that the cyclical component isn't there," says University of Michigan economist Betsey Stevenson. "It's that the aging component is there and growing" (Leubsdorf, 2016).

Emerging Trend #3: Teaching Data Analytics Skills

As more and more industries get the technology treatment—that layer of technology that upends business as usual—data analytics will make its way into most every company department, directly or otherwise. Data analytics—evaluating data using analytical and logical reasoning to form a conclusion and/or prediction—and statistics will become ever more prominently and pervasively used in most industries. Technical writing and reading will be key skills. Students must learn how to speak clearly and listen attentively and in technical terms.

Consider, again, the automotive industry. Auto technicians in the near future will need to understand a car's computer programming and code. Data analytics and statistics are not yet part of any auto tech curriculum, but trends tell us they should be.

Data analysis is a skill in high demand. It was the top job for 2016, and based on hiring demand and the potential for salary growth, it's poised to remain a top job for the foreseeable future (Dishman, 2016a). Even more, as of January 2016, there were 1,736 data scientist openings with a median base salary of $116,840 (Dishman, 2016b).

How are we going to fill the demand if we're not teaching these foundational, in-demand skills starting in K-12 curriculum? What kinds of jobs, we must ask, will our graduates be qualified to do if not the high-skilled, high-paying ones of the technology-driven economy?

Students' success beyond school will depend ever more on creating, evaluating, and analyzing material, while applying solutions to real-world, unpredictable situations, with multiple possible solutions. In other words, it will depend on what they can do with what they know.

Emerging Trend #4: New Technology-Based Tools to Deliver Instruction

"Sage on the stage" teaching is so twentieth (and nineteenth) century!

Welcome to computer games, or the gamification of learning. Welcome to Google Cardboard and Oculus Rift. Welcome to virtual reality and augmented reality—VR and AR. What are we talking about?

Gamification or *digital game-based learning* (DGBL) is an educational tool to motivate students and enhance engagement and learning through the use of digital video game design and game elements. DGBL is typically adaptive, meaning it can adjust the difficulty level of the tasks it presents to the users/learners based on their performance. Learning is then customized and individualized, matching learners with their own needs and ability levels. The goal is to inspire and motivate students to continue learning because the games are fun and challenging.

Currently, there are more than half a billion people worldwide playing online games at least an hour a day; 183 million in the United States alone, says Jane McGonigal, author of *Reality Is Broken: Why*

Games Make Us Better and How They Can Change the World. She says the younger you are, the more likely you are to be a "gamer"; 97 percent of boys and 94 percent of girls under the age of 18 report playing video games regularly. The average young person, McGonigal says, racks up 10,000 hours of gaming by the time they turn 21. That's exactly as much time as they spend in a classroom during all of middle school and high school, if they have perfect attendance. Most astonishingly, five million gamers in the United States are spending more than 40 hours a week playing games—the same as a full-time job (McGonigal, 2011)!

Virtual reality (VR) is infiltrating more and more classrooms to bring learning to life. At least the easy-to-assemble and more affordable VR tools, like Google Cardboard, have begun to crop up in classrooms across the country.

Google Cardboard is a VR device used with a head mount for a smartphone. It is named for its fold-over cardboard viewer. Through the end of 2015 and into 2016, Google had shipped five million viewers and developed more than one thousand applications. With costs for one Google Cardboard kit ranging between $10 and $40, they are within reach for many school budgets.

Google Cardboard is being used to (virtually) break down the walls of classrooms and transport students to different worlds and times. Studying hurricanes? Google Cardboard can take students into the eye of the storm. Learning about the Renaissance? Google Cardboard can let students time travel to other centuries and environments, lifting learning from the textbook and into vivid life.

The company Oculus wants to "make it possible for you to experience anything, anywhere." The Oculus Rift is a next-generation VR system. "Rift is unlike anything you've ever experienced," the company's website notes. "Whether you're stepping into your favorite game, watching an immersive VR movie, jumping to a destination on the other side of the world, or just spending time with friends in VR, you'll feel like you're really there."

In the summer of 2015, the University of Michigan became the first university in the country to start using VR in its football program. Athletic administrators wanted to provide behind-the-scenes content that immersed prospective recruits in its football facilities to give a sense of what a typical Saturday game-day environment is like at Michigan Stadium.

At a meeting with Michigan football players and coaches before the 2015 season, Taylor Kavanaugh of Headcase, a Los Angeles VR company, demonstrated the company's custom-made headset. Headcase had created several pieces of VR content. One focused on "a day in the life of a Michigan football player." Another explored the "Michigan game-day experience." During recruiting, prospects often ask coaches and players what it's like to play football at Michigan. With the headset and content, they have an answer they can fully experience. It's not quite a campus visit, but it's getting close.

This kind of technological innovation is happening in other fields as well. In 2015, the *New York Times* partnered with Google to develop an app for readers to experience stories through VR. *USA Today* followed suit in 2016, and more newspapers and magazines will follow these leaders. The objective is to provide an immersive and personalized experience.

Online education courses are exploding across the country. For example, K12 Inc., founded in 1999, is the number one provider of K-12 online education classes. The company generates $1 billion in sales from its online courses. A growing number of public schools across the country are adopting online curriculum to create an individualized learning approach in the traditional classroom. The country's largest educational publishers are working with online education companies to change how instructional materials and learning resources are developed and delivered.

A key question for educators is this: Are we going to bring online courses into our schools, or draw a line in the sand and keep them out? My view is let's bring them in and let them do what they do best—personalize instruction, allowing students to work at their own pace. In turn, teachers will be freed to do what they do best—strengthen relationships, encourage individuals, and support the development of the personal and interpersonal skills of their students. This will go a long way toward helping create productive, conscientious, and engaged citizens, not to mention highly sought-after employees.

Each of these technology tools and resources deserves the attention of all educators. Each has the potential to increase rigor, relevance, and engagement for all learners.

Emerging Trend # 5: Professional Development for New Instructional Frontiers

The first few trends are a lot to digest. Hopefully there can be comfort in our final trend: professional development. Given the first four trends, educators will be asking teachers to teach in ways for which there is little precedent. Yet in asking this of teachers, they automatically deserve the support of their leaders. And their leaders, mind you, need and deserve support, as well.

There's a saying about change: everyone's in favor of change...until it involves you. That's the challenge: Some will welcome change. Others will resist even trying to use new forms of instruction in new ways.

Remember that change is most tolerable when it is evolutionary, not revolutionary. Begin first with that one third of people who are willing to try. They will bring along the one third who are fence sitters. The final third gradually will realize that they need to either get with the program or move on.

Teachers will need time and a safe environment to learn about, observe, practice, and develop the new skills required for a novel, but necessary, way of teaching. Only through a system that supports teacher and leadership development, collaboration, and professional practices will schools create transformed and transformative learning environments that result in improved student achievement.

A Current View of the Career Landscape

Another practice we make a habit of at ICLE is analyzing labor and employment data. Doing so helps us stay current on which job sectors are seeing shrinking employment and why. This information helps bring accuracy to our stake-in-the-ground predictions. After all, if a job sector or industry is under assault by technology, there's little use in teaching the specific skills it requires to our students. On the other hand, if a job sector or industry is showing upward momentum, then we'd be wise to incorporate the skills it requires into learning.

Information like this is empowering and helpful. If you are unwilling or unable to keep track of employment data, trends, and insights, seek someone on your team who will do so eagerly and regularly.

To be of service to you now, what follows is a catalog of jobs and industries our research has shown are shrinking and growing, as well as general employment trends. And then there is an overview of jobs and industries posting strong growth and a list of the skills they will require. Take this catalog into your meetings as you plan your educational programming with colleagues.

Shrinking Jobs and Industries

As we know, middle class jobs are disappearing at an alarming rate. Specifically, middle class jobs that are projected to take a hit in the coming years range from office-related occupations, such as couriers and messengers, data entry positions, and switchboard operators to light manufacturing machinists. Even newer technology jobs, such as computer operators, are being replaced by improved software and processes. A lot of these jobs are disappearing because of the increased use of the Internet and company intranets (Lieberman, 2015).

Other occupations whose numbers are likely to contract involve jobs that are increasingly being done by customers. For example, as airlines encourage travelers to make their own reservations and print their own tickets, the number of ticketing agents will shrink considerably, tracking the loss of travel agent jobs. This trend will spread to other fields, like entertainment, where customers can book their own tickets and manage their own reservations online (Lieberman, 2015).

In their 2013 paper "The Future of Employment," Carl Frey and Michael Osborne argued that jobs are in high risk of being automated in 47 percent of the occupational categories into which work is sorted. A partial list includes telemarketers, secretarial and administrative assistants, accountants and auditors, technical writers, machinists, and economists, among others (Frey & Osborne, 2013).

The combination of big data and smart machines will take over some occupations outright. In others, it will allow companies to do more with fewer workers. For example, text-mining programs will displace professional jobs in legal services. Biopsies will be analyzed more efficiently by image-processing software than by lab technicians. Machines are already turning basic sports results and financial data into news stories. Keep an eye on other industries that will take this hit. Will there be airline pilots? Or traffic cops? Or soldiers?

Growing Jobs and Industries

To win well-paying jobs of the future, workers must be more effective and adept than machines. They will need to competently and flexibly use a mix of technical knowledge and noncognitive skills to bring value to employers.

More careers will continue to be created in entrepreneurial companies than at large corporations. As we know, these jobs require certain attitudes, mindsets, and behaviors to navigate both less structured environments and less obvious career paths.

In specific terms, according to the Bureau of Labor Statistics' report on the fastest-growing occupations between 2014 and 2024, 81 percent of job growth will be in service-providing sectors. Healthcare and social assistance jobs will account for over a third of the jobs added in this period (Bureau of Labor Statistics, 2016). Success in these roles will often rely heavily on strong interpersonal and noncognitive skills. And on the more technical side of healthcare jobs, success will also require data analytics skills.

Outside of the healthcare and social assistance categories, jobs that will also see significant growth through 2024 include statisticians, operations research analysts, personal financial advisors, cartographers and photogrammetrists, interpreters and translators, forensic science technicians, and web developers (Bureau of Labor Statistics, 2016). All of these jobs necessitate agility and fluency with data and robust analytical skills. Those who occupy these roles will also need to know how to take or advise action with the data they collect, monitor, investigate, or evaluate.

Key Skills for Our Changing Workplace

Based on where jobs are heading in the next decade, these are the skills that need to be addressed in our classrooms today:

- Students will need to analyze vast amounts of data quickly and efficiently. To do that, schools must start teaching data analytics, which is simply evaluating data using analytical and logical reasoning to form a finding or conclusion.
- Students increasingly will need to communicate through charts, tables, and graphs. We've got to teach kids how to understand tables, graphs, and charts and how to build them, especially in the workplace.
- Students will need to know basic statistics. Today, statistics is typically not taught until college. But in looking at employment trends, we know this won't cut it anymore. Figure out how you can integrate statistics into your math curriculum in K–12, and then make it a new core subject in high school mathematics. Consider where else statistics pop up—sociology, biology, history, to name just some subjects—and take an interdisciplinary approach to its incorporation for added real-world relevance and interest for students.
- Because we live in such a technologically rich environment, the ability for technical reading and technical writing will be critical for all students.
- Voice recognition software also will improve dramatically in the immediate future. Virtual assistants Siri, Cortana, and the others will become very, very precise. That means students must learn how to speak clearly and in technical terms—in other words, technical speaking. And that's not taught at all. You might get it indirectly if you take many engineering courses, but it's not being taught to everybody.

In short, success and self-sufficiency will increasingly depend on creating, evaluating, and analyzing material and applying solutions to real-world, unpredictable situations.

Chapter Nine

The Rigor/Relevance Framework®

Establishing a Career- and College-Ready Instructional Program

To be ready for college means to be ready to deepen area expertise. To be ready for today's careers means to have an interdisciplinary view of subjects and the capacity to apply that knowledge to a variety of circumstances, predictable or otherwise. Career ready means moving from mere knowledge acquisition to knowledge application. Knowledge gathering is vital, do not get me wrong. But it's just not enough for twenty-first-century careers.

I created the Rigor/Relevance Framework® specifically to push instruction through both knowledge acquisition and knowledge application. Schools that organize their instructional programs around the Framework see great success in preparing students with both the academic and application skills they must have to be career ready. The Framework functions both as a planning tool to examine curriculum, instruction, and assessment, and as an embedded, career-ready vetting tool. The Framework automatically prompts teachers to check for instruction that utilizes both higher levels of thinking and challenging application opportunities.

The Rigor/Relevance Framework®

The Framework is based on two dimensions: higher levels of "knowing" and increasingly complex levels of "doing."

First, a vertical continuum of knowledge describes the increasingly complex ways in which we think. This so-called Knowledge Taxonomy is based on the six levels of the Revised Bloom's Taxonomy:

6. Creating
5. Evaluating
4. Analyzing
3. Applying
2. Understanding
1. Remembering

Thinking Continuum

Acquisition of Knowledge ➡ **Assimilation** of Knowledge

The lower end of this continuum involves identifying, acquiring, or recalling knowledge and recalling or locating that knowledge in a simple manner. Just as a computer completes a word search in a word processing program, a competent person at this level can scan thousands of bits of information in his or her brain to locate that desired knowledge.

The high end of the Knowledge Taxonomy addresses more complex ways in which individuals use knowledge. At this level, knowledge is fully integrated in one's mind, and individuals can do much more than locate or remember information—they can take several pieces of knowledge and combine them in logical and creative ways. *Assimilation of knowledge* is an accurate way to describe this more complex level of thinking. Assimilation is typically considered a higher-order thinking skill; at this level, students can solve multi-step problems, create unique work, and devise solutions.

We call the second continuum the "Application Model," which includes five levels:

1. Knowledge in one discipline
2. Apply in discipline
3. Apply across disciplines
4. Apply to real-world predictable situations
5. Apply to real-world unpredictable situations

This model puts knowledge to use. While the low end is knowledge acquired for its own sake, the high end signifies action—using that knowledge to solve complex, real-world problems while creating projects, designs, and other works for use in real-world situations.

Rigor/Relevance Framework®

The Rigor/Relevance Framework® has four quadrants.

- *Quadrant A* represents simple recall and basic acquisition and understanding of knowledge for its own sake. Quadrant C represents more complex thinking, but still knowledge for its own sake. Examples of Quadrant A knowledge are knowing that the world is round and that Shakespeare wrote *Hamlet*.
- *Quadrant C* embraces higher levels of knowledge, such as knowing how the U.S. political system works and analyzing the benefits and challenges of this country's cultural diversity versus those of other nations to create new understandings.

- *Quadrants B and D* represent action or high and low degrees of application. Quadrant B would include knowing how to use math skills to make purchases and count change. The ability to access information in network systems and the ability to gather knowledge from different sources to solve a complex workplace or scientific problems, many with multiple possible solutions, are types of Quadrant D thinking and doing.

Each of these four quadrants can also be labeled with a term that characterizes student performance.

- **Quadrant A: Acquisition.** Students gather and store bits of knowledge and information. Teachers expect students to remember or understand this acquired knowledge.
- **Quadrant B: Application.** Students use acquired knowledge to solve less complex problems, design solutions, and complete more routine work (compared to the highest level of application, which is more typically Quadrant D: applying appropriate knowledge to new and unpredictable situations).
- **Quadrant C: Assimilation.** Students extend and refine their acquired knowledge to automatically and routinely analyze and solve more complex problems, sometimes creating unique solutions.
- **Quadrant D: Adaptation.** Students have the competence to think in complex ways and apply the knowledge and skills they have acquired. Even when confronted with perplexing unknowns and multiple possible approaches, students are able to use their extensive knowledge to create solutions and take action that further develops their skills and knowledge.

The Rigor/Relevance Framework® is a fresh approach to college- and career-ready standards and assessment. It is based on traditional elements of education, yet encourages the shift from acquisition of knowledge to application of knowledge.

The Framework is easy to understand. With its simple, straightforward structure, it can serve as a bridge between the school and the community. It's a vehicle to provide a more rigorous and relevant curriculum, while encompassing much of what parents, business leaders, and community members want students to learn and learn to do.

The Framework is also versatile: educators can use it to develop instruction and assessment. Likewise, teachers can measure their progress in adding rigor and relevance to instruction, while selecting appropriate instructional strategies to meet learner needs and higher achievement goals.

The Rigor/Relevance Framework® in Action: A Student Performance Example

What follows is an example of student performance at different levels of knowledge acquisition and application.

The expected achievement level for teaching "nutrition" can vary depending on the purpose of the instruction. If a teacher only wants students to acquire basic nutritional knowledge, student performance set at level 1 or 2 on the Knowledge Taxonomy (see following chart) is adequate. If the teacher wants students to understand the concept more deeply, then some objectives need to be similar to levels 4 through 6.

Basic Nutrition—Knowledge

Level	Performance
1. Remembering	Label foods by nutritional groups.
2. Understanding	Explain nutritional value of individual foods.
3. Applying	Make use of nutritional guidelines when planning meals.
4. Analyzing	Examine success in achieving nutritional goals.
5. Evaluating	Appraise results of personal eating habits over time.
6. Creating	Develop personal nutritional goals.

Note that each of the levels requires students to think differently. Levels 4–6 require more complex thinking than levels 1–3.

Defining the level of relevance in curriculum and instructional activities is a little more difficult than determining the Knowledge Taxonomy level. However, just as the Knowledge Taxonomy categorizes increasing levels of thinking, the Application Model describes increasingly complex applications and uses of knowledge. Any student performance can be expressed as one of five levels in the Application Model.

The following basic nutrition example is similar to the Knowledge Taxonomy one, in that it uses nutrition to describe student performance at various levels. However in this Application Model example, each level requires students to *apply* knowledge differently.

Basic Nutrition—Application

Level	Performance
1. Knowledge in One Discipline	Label foods by nutritional groups.
2. Application in One Discipline	Rank foods by nutritional value.
3. Interdisciplinary Application	Make cost comparisons of different foods considering nutritional value.
4. Real-World Predictable Situations	Develop a nutritional plan for a person with a health problem affected by food intake.
5. Real-World Unpredictable Applications	Devise a sound nutritional plan for a group of 3-year-olds who are picky eaters.

Also similar to the first example, the expected achievement level for teaching nutrition can vary depending on the purpose of the instruction. If a teacher wants students only to apply basic nutritional knowledge, student performance set at level 1 is adequate. If the teacher wants students to apply knowledge of nutrition significantly further, then objectives may need to be at levels 4 and 5.

A Shift in How We Teach

Getting students from quadrants A and C to quadrants B and D sounds straightforward. The truth is that it can be a tough climb for schools, but it has a summit that can and will be highly rewarding.

Many educators are regulated, certified, valued, and tenured around quadrants A and C. Teacher training, report cards—virtually all academic traditions—are typically established around A/C learning. Getting to quadrants B and D instead will require a significant paradigm shift.

In A/C, teachers are typically at the front of their classrooms disseminating knowledge. They are at the center of the wheel. Classrooms where these teachers teach often look the same, with row upon row of desks and chairs. The teacher is the "center stage" dispenser of knowledge.

The role of the teacher changes dramatically in a B/D setting. There, the teacher becomes a facilitator, coach, and enabler.

What exactly does that mean? Let's look at it this way: at some point in their careers, many teachers probably coached a sport or got involved in the performing arts. Think how differently a coach coaches or a performing arts director directs. It's all about application. It's all about getting students ready to perform. Teachers in those positions aren't actually on the stage or on the field. Rather, they are on the sidelines, off-stage, directing. They are facilitators and motivators.

This example represents a shift away from teaching and a move toward learning. Put another way, educators should be starting to ask this crucial question: What do we want students to be able to actually *do*?

The transition from teaching to facilitating will succeed only with a huge dose of mindset shift and professional development along these lines.

A Shift in How Administrators Approach Change

It's not enough to ask teachers to teach differently and provide the corresponding training. Administrators can schedule as much professional development time as teachers can handle, but fundamental, lasting change won't occur unless administrators change, as well.

To get to B/D, administrators must make adjustments in themselves. They must learn to think differently. They must learn to become managers of the change process. That's a foreign concept to many district and building leaders whose training prepared them to manage (and preserve) a structure, but not to change the structure. Leaders, too, deserve and will benefit from executive coaching sessions around how to implement and manage change—successfully.

A Shift in Classrooms to Support B/D Learning

Finally, to successfully get to B/D, educators must reimagine their physical classrooms and teaching spaces.

Twenty-first-century spaces should create an environment that is exciting for students, while helping to shift the focus from a "teacher-centered" to a "learner-centered" culture. Classroom design should enable highly interactive instruction and collaboration, thus letting teachers bring relevancy to daily instruction.

A dynamic instructional program requires flexible classrooms that adapt to a learner-centered environment. Replacing current furniture, for example, with modular contemporary furniture will help create that environment.

Chapter Ten

The Daggett System for Effective Instruction

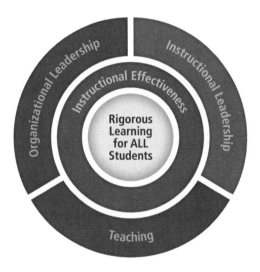

Pairing Research with Best Practices

During the past 25 years, we at ICLE have had the privilege of studying and working with hundreds of our nation's most rapidly improving schools. Each one is committed to improving the performance of all its students. This work has taught us that school improvement is not an event, but a process. It involves a classroom-to-boardroom approach. To help guide that work, we created the Daggett System for Effective Instruction (DSEI). This framework can help you put in place those changes needed to prepare all of your students with the academic and knowledge application skills to be both career and college ready.

DSEI relies on two key approaches:

1. A comprehensive review of research focused on effective schools in general, and effective instruction in particular.
2. A careful analysis of the best practices we observed in the nation's most rapidly improving schools.

Key Research Behind DSEI

Recognizing the challenges facing schools today is easy. Identifying the most effective ways to address them is not. Education research is plentiful and comprehensive, so much so that studies are available to prove or disprove almost any decision made by educational leadership. However, most of the respected research is consistent on one key school improvement issue: *Effective instruction really matters*. No single variable has more impact than teaching.

The following research serves as the foundation to DSEI.

Hattie's Visible Learning

John Hattie's book, *Visible Learning: A Synthesis of Over 800 Meta-Analyses Relating to Achievement*, is a key influence on DSEI. Hattie analyzed 200,000 "effect sizes" (the relative impact of one factor compared to other factors) from 52,637 studies involving more than 50 million students and covering an exhaustive number of factors (Hattie, 2008).

Hattie's approach was that effect sizes are the best way to identify what has the greatest influence on student learning. The calculations behind his work are complex, but to simplify, an "effect size" of 1.0 (defined as an increase of one standard deviation) is typically associated with the equivalent of approximately two years of learner growth in one year.

His analysis shows that most variables in schools have an effect size of around +0.3 or +0.4, what Hattie calls the "hinge point." Any factor below +0.4 is of lower value. Factors below 0.0 have negative effects. Some factors can be directly affected by an education organization; others cannot. Some noteworthy effect sizes from his research include:

- Formative Evaluation: +0.90 (approximately 1.7 years of growth)
- Providing Feedback: +0.73 (approximately 1.44 years of growth)
- Student Teacher Relationships: +0.72 (approximately 1.44 years of growth)
- Prior Achievement: +0.67 (approximately 1.34 years of growth)
- Professional Development: +0.62 (approximately 1.24 years of growth)
- Socioeconomic Status: +0.57 (approximately 1.14 years of growth)
- Peer Tutoring: +0.55 (approximately 1.13 years of growth)
- Teaching Test-Taking: +0.22 (approximately 1.03 years of growth)
- Reducing Class Size: +0.21 (approximately 1.03 years of growth)

On the other hand, certain factors have negative impact:

- Mobility: −0.68 (approximately 1.34 years of loss)

InTASC Model Core Teaching Standards
Another publication that influenced DSEI is *InTASC Model Core Teaching Standards: A Resource for State Dialogue.* Developed by the Council of Chief State School Officers (CCSSO), this book outlines the common principles and foundations of teaching practices that cut across all subject areas and grade levels, and that are necessary to improve student achievement (CCSSO, 2011).

Sutton Trust Toolkit of Strategies to Improve Learning
The goal of this United Kingdom study, published in May 2011, was to help schools determine which research-proven instructional practices were most effective in supporting students from economically disadvantaged backgrounds (Higgins, Kokotsaki, & Coe, 2011). They also analyzed each instructional practice's levels of relative costs, even though there "is no direct link between spending on schools and outcomes for pupils." The findings closely parallel Hattie's meta-analysis of instructional effectiveness and also reflect the intent of the International Center's Efficiency and Effectiveness Framework,

correlating effectiveness and cost, which is described later in this chapter.

The Work of Robert Marzano

Robert Marzano's extensive work focuses mainly on instruction. Insights from his paper, "41 Key Strategies Identified by Research for Effective Teaching and What Works in Schools: Translating Research into Action," are core to DSEI. As he states in *The Art and Science of Teaching,* "No amount of further research will provide an airtight model of instruction...The best research can do is tell us which strategies have a good chance (i.e., high probability) of working well with students" (Marzano, 2007).

Charlotte Danielson's The Framework for Teaching

The Framework for Teaching is a research-based set of components of instruction that divides the complex activity of teaching into 22 components (Danielson, 2007). It also helped inform DSEI.

Focused on Student Success: A Five-Year Research Study of Models, Networks, and Policies

The not-for-profit Successful Practices Network (for which I serve as Chairman) and the Council of Chief State School Officers (the organization representing each state's most senior education official) joined forces to conduct a five-year study on the models, networks, and policies that best support and sustain rigor and relevance for *all* students. It was made possible through a generous grant from the Bill & Melinda Gates Foundation.

The study revealed five key findings, all of which were used in the development of DSEI (Lucey, Silver, Corso, & Fox, 2010):

1. *Leadership*: A clear sense of purpose that empowers staff toward a common vision.
2. *High expectations:* For academic performance as well as college/career readiness.
3. *Relationships:* Valuing relationships as part of a successful learning environment.

4. *Student opportunities:* Both academic "stretch" and personal skill development opportunities.
5. *Professional culture:* Teachers, administration, and staff collaborate toward goals.

Collectively, our broad research base, a purposeful focus on the aforementioned six studies, and insights from several outstanding education thought leaders catalyzed our thinking and then our shaping of DSEI.

We focused DSEI on "teaching" because the research supports what most educators know in their hearts: What goes on between a teacher and a student is central to high-level learning. Effective teaching is a means to an end, a belief that all kids can learn. And all means *all!*

Achieving this goal requires a system—a supportive and aligned system. Put another way, although teaching is essential, by itself it is not enough to ensure rigorous learning for all students. The need for an organization-wide commitment is at the heart of DSEI.

The Daggett System for Effective Instruction

For decades, the International Center has been an active participant in helping to transform schools. Our on-the-ground work has reinforced the idea that it takes a system to develop, maintain, and enhance effective instruction, which ultimately leads to rigorous and relevant learning. In the end, instructional and organizational leadership must support teaching.

DSEI has also been significantly influenced by these factors:

*   **Observing and disseminating best practices.** For 25 years, the International Center has assisted teachers and school leadership, along with identifying, studying, and showcasing America's most successful schools.
*   **Current and past research** conducted by some of the most respected thought leaders in K–12 education.

At the same time, DSEI departs from existing models and frameworks in several significant ways:

Traditional Teaching Frameworks	Daggett System for Effective Instruction
What teachers should do	What the entire system should do
Teacher-focused	Student-focused
Teachers deliver instruction	Teachers facilitate learning
Vision is set by top leaders	Vision is built more inclusively
Define vision primarily in terms of academic measures	Define vision as strong academics and personal skills and the ability to apply them
Rigid structures support adult needs	Flexible structures support student needs
Focus on teaching	Focus on learning

Other models are excellent guides and tools for what they choose to focus on, primarily teachers' professional development, mastery of content, and use of instructional strategies.

By comparison, DSEI's most distinguishing attributes include:

- A focus on coherence and alignment at the system/organization level.
- A focus on instructional leadership grounded in a broad base of analysis and meta-analysis research on instructional effectiveness and rigorous learning.
- Balancing effectiveness with considerations of efficacy (e.g., affordability).
- Best practices drawn from observing and partnering with model schools.

DSEI leverages more than the teacher in the classroom. Its keys to success include an emphasis on vertical alignment, through organizational systems and structures, along with instructional leadership, and horizontal alignment.

The system must be focused on making teachers optimally effective because teachers are the most powerful influence on students and instruction. DSEI provides a coherent focus across the entire education system: Organizational Leadership, Institutional Leadership, and most importantly, Teaching. The remaining pages of this chapter well describe what the nation's most rapidly improving schools have done to address each of these areas.

Organizational Leadership

Organizational Leadership is a function, not just a person. It involves a mentality, structure, focus, and commitment to create the environment in which learning is optimized. Six primary elements of Organizational Leadership follow.

1. **Create a culture of high academic expectations and positive relationships.** That culture must communicate and encompass several questions:

   - *Why:* The challenges of changing demographics and a wired and tech-savvy generation of students growing up in a digital world; a global economy, in which America must innovate and compete; technology transforming and/or threatening multiple industries and jobs.
   - *To Whom:* Students, staff, and community stakeholders.
   - *How:* Through active and ongoing communications and messaging at staff development events, community forums, business roundtables, and so on.

2. **Establish a shared vision and communicate to all constituent groups.** Organizational Leadership must determine core beliefs and values that can establish a shared vision of student success. Vision must ultimately support the instructional effectiveness and positive relationships that lead to a culture of high expectations, and then all goals and plans should be aligned to it. Organizational leaders are responsible for communicating vision and aligned action plans in a way that all stakeholders can understand, contribute to, and commit to.

   The International Center's Learning Criteria (http://leadered. com/our-philosophy/learning-criteria.php) is a broad, holistic framework of variables and a useful resource for helping turn school culture into a shared vision and definition of student success, not just as scholars, but as future workers, citizens, consumers, and parents.

3. **Align organizational structures and systems to the vision.** After organizational leaders have established culture and mission, they must communicate that there is a cohesive structure/system in place supporting the established vision, goals, and action items. Organizational leaders must effectively bridge the system, from central office administration down through teachers' ranks, connecting the development, alignment, adoption, and integration of the curriculum into instruction. They must also align the vision and structures to ensure literacy and math integration across all grade levels and disciplines.

   Using the International Center's Effectiveness and Efficiency Framework (http://leadered.com/our-philosophy/effectiveness-efficiency.php), DSEI extends the data and research on effectiveness. It allows decision makers to consider the broader perspective of how to prioritize initiatives for enhancing instructional effectiveness and then examining both effectiveness and efficiency. For example, when organizational leaders analyze a few of John Hattie's factors using the Effectiveness and Efficiency Framework, they can not only see that they are effective, but also make efficient use of resources to provide the highest "return on investment."

	Effect (Standard Deviation) 1 Standard Deviation = ~2 years growth	Relative Cost
Student-Teacher Relationships	.72 (11)	Low
Application of Knowledge	.65 (17)	Low
Professional Development	.62 (19)	Low

4. **Build leadership capacity through an empowerment model.** Organizational Leadership must enhance the competencies of existing leaders and also help develop future leaders. Doing so broadens the leadership capacity of the organization

immediately and paves the way for continuous development of new leaders who can assist in transforming a school or district. Empowering others to lead around action items not only builds the capacity to complete goals, but also builds the capacity of others to lead and adapt to every changing need. Creating an empowered environment demands clear communication and collaboration at all levels, in turn creating trust among members of the organization.

5. **Align teacher/leader selection, support, and evaluation.** Organizational leaders must focus on building the capacity of both teachers and instructional leaders, which is essential to the growth of individuals within an organization. A formative approach provides the best opportunity for teachers and leaders to successfully reach their personal and professional goals which, in turn, helps the organization reach its goals. Focusing on the formative process provides opportunity for feedback and constructive professional learning that leads to successfully meeting the evaluation criteria.

6. **Support decision making with relevant data systems.** Organizational leaders must ensure that easy-to-use data systems are built, and then provide training at all levels. Meaningful data systems are the key to monitoring student improvement and progress toward goals, while also informing instruction. Organizational leaders must monitor and ensure the system is used effectively at all levels and that the data provides opportunities for deep conversations about student achievement, teacher growth, and reaching goals.

Instructional Leadership

Instructional Leadership must focus on instructional effectiveness and ultimately rigorous learning for *all* students. A variety of people can provide Instructional Leadership to support teachers, including:

- District and regional instructional leadership
- Principals, assistant principals
- Department chairs, teacher leaders

- Expert teachers, counselors, social workers
- Mentor teachers, teacher coaches, teaching peers/team leaders

The Instructional Leadership segment of the Daggett System concentrates on six overarching elements:

1. **Use research and establish the urgent need for change to promote higher academic expectations and positive relationships.** The first job of Instructional Leadership is to reinforce the vision set forth by Organizational Leadership. To do so, Instructional Leadership must clearly communicate to all constituents the process that will be used for change. As part of this communication, Instructional leaders must offer "proof statements" to staff, students, and stakeholders; i.e., research and authoritative testimony that corroborate the need to improve student achievement. ICLE's Essential Skills Study and its research on reading and math proficiency levels involving the Lexile® Framework for Reading and Quantile® Framework for Mathematics are examples of such indicators. Instructional leaders also must see themselves as the essential "change agents" in raising standards and expectations.

2. **Develop, implement, and monitor standards-aligned curriculum and assessments.** Instructional leaders are charged with implementing a curriculum and instruction process that engages teachers and key leaders while assuring a tight connection between aligned standards and instruction and assessment. Instructional leaders must prepare teachers for instruction and formative assessments. They also are responsible for monitoring the process to ensure that standards are aligned and that instruction and assessment reflect the adopted curriculum.

3. **Integrate literacy, math, and technology across all disciplines.** Literacy, math, and the ability to navigate technology are enabling skills that are essential across all disciplines and for success in college and careers. All teachers at all grades and across all subjects need to assume responsibility for this

heightened emphasis on broad-based literacy development. Similarly, math must focus on problem solving, reasoning, and proof, along with so-called "strands of mathematical proficiency" (including adaptive reasoning, strategic competence, conceptual understanding, procedural fluency, and productive disposition). Therefore, Instructional Leadership must ensure that the integration and application of math and literacy standards across all disciplines are supported, implemented, and monitored.

4. **Facilitate data-driven decision-making to inform instruction.** To meet the needs of diverse learners, Instructional Leaders must provide relevant data to educators. Educators, in turn, will access the information and analyze trends toward district and school goals, monitor learner progress, and differentiate instruction based on student needs. Instructional leaders must put systems in place to provide teachers with a clearer understanding of student data and how to apply that understanding to actionable instruction and interventions. They must also install systems to monitor the effective use of data.

5. **Provide opportunities for professional learning, collaboration, and growth focused on high-quality instruction and increased student learning.** The research conducted by Hattie and others clearly shows the importance of teacher selection and development, along with a continuous cycle of evaluation and support. Professional development should be a cornerstone. With an effect factor of .62 (the equivalent of approximately 1.24 years of growth) on Hattie's scale, professional development is a high-impact and cost-effective approach to improving instructional effectiveness for student achievement (Hattie, 2008).

   Instructional leaders must use the most relevant data and research to determine the professional learning needs of the district or the school. They must find ways to implement professional learning that maximizes growth of individuals, and then track increased learner achievement. Professional learning should target and support both the foundations of effective instruction and the foundations of effective leadership that support effective instruction.

6. **Engage families and community in the learning process.** Several studies show that when family members and the community are engaged in schools, student achievement climbs. This generally happens across the board. The challenge is figuring out how to get families involved when more and more parents work full-time or have language barriers or other challenges that might make it difficult to get involved. Innovative schools are finding creative ways for parents to engage in their children's learning. They are also developing initiatives to forge stronger ties to the community so students feel consistent support.

Teaching

If Organizational Leadership and Instructional Leadership do their jobs effectively, then the vanguard of rigorous and relevant learning—effective teaching—will be well supported in addressing the daunting challenges of the classroom.

Drawing on research about teacher effectiveness and observations of best practices for more than two decades, DSEI includes the following six broad elements under Teaching.

1. **Build effective instruction based on rigorous and relevant expectations.** Teachers must embrace the organizational vision that all students can and will learn, and must strive to help every student reach his or her fullest potential. This is the attitude that effective teachers bring to class every day. Embracing high expectations is an offshoot of commitment and caring for individual students. The equivalent "success criteria" factors in Hattie's analysis, "Mastery Learning" and "Feedback," indicate effectiveness factors of +0.53 and +0.73, respectively (Hattie, 2008). Teachers must learn how to translate content knowledge into effective instructional strategies relevant to the learner.

2. **Create and implement an effective learner environment that is engaging and aligned to learner needs.** Teachers must create a

learning environment that addresses students' personal, social, and emotional needs. The environment must engage all learners; therefore, environment plays a key role in student success. Teachers also must develop positive relationships with students, allowing them to know each individual student. The presence of strong relationships between students and teachers builds trust that positively impacts learning and the learning environment. Hattie places "Student-Teacher Relationships" at +0.72, or approximately the impact of nearly a year and a half of growth every school year (Hattie, 2008).

3. **Possess and continue to develop content area knowledge and make it relevant to the learner.** Teachers, with the support of the system, must stay current with the most effective pedagogy, the most contemporary content, and the most relevant experiences that connect back to content. While teachers must have strong content expertise in the subjects they teach, effective instruction is more than just transmitting knowledge. It is equally the ability to make connections, show relevance, nurture engagement, and embed understanding.

4. **Plan and provide learning experiences using effective research-based strategies that are embedded with best practices, including the use of technology.** Every teacher needs a thorough understanding of pedagogy as well as a versatile and comprehensive repertoire of instructional strategies— classic and innovative—to draw from in planning and providing instruction so they can match teaching approaches with learning objectives, subject matter, and targeted learners. Teachers must plan and provide learning experiences at high levels of rigor and relevance. Lessons must be tightly aligned to appropriate standards. Effective strategies and the use of technology must be embedded in all learning experiences to give all students access to the material.

Teachers also need a clear understanding of today's students who are "wired differently," who want to see a reason for learning something, who fascinate their elders with their technology skills (in fact, they take connectivity and instant access to information and to one another for granted), who multi-task, and, perhaps most significantly, who would rather do to learn than learn to do. They collaborate naturally and seamlessly. Not surprisingly, they simply learn differently. The abundance of recent discoveries in neuropsychology and brain research can and should inform teachers' understanding of twenty-first-century learners.

5. **Use assessment and data to guide and differentiate instruction.** Good teachers always ask themselves: Did they all get it? How do I know they got it? How do I measure mastery? How do I help those students who didn't? How do I know at any given point in the year if students are on track to grow and achieve? Teachers must use effective assessments to collect relevant data to make decisions on teaching and learning. Teachers must also be able to differentiate and adapt instruction based on the needs of the class and individual students, while using data to track student growth. Hattie's meta-analysis rates the use of formative assessment data to inform instruction as the number one factor in instructional effectiveness, finding its rating to be +0.90, or almost two full years of growth in a single year.

6. **Further content and instructional knowledge through continuous professional learning that is both enriching and collaborative.** The professional development opportunities needed to support teachers in today's learning environments are huge and will not be met with traditional workshops or unfocused staff-development days. Teachers will need time and a safe environment to practice and develop the skills of effective instruction. Many will need coaches working with them in the classroom to model best practices. They will need time for reflection with their peers in order to make best practices part of their repertoire of skills. Fortunately, most teachers value, expect, and welcome meaningful professional development that is directly related to their work, is based on current research and best practices, and meets their individual needs.

Teachers must be supported in continuous growth toward accessing and using the best instructional strategies and integrating technology into lessons. Through a systemic approach, they must also have access to a highly collaborative environment that empowers them to be leaders in developing and sharing effective practices. Only through a system that supports teacher development, collaboration, and professional practices will teachers be able to deliver learning environments that result in improved rigorous learning for all students.

Summary

The Daggett System for Effective Instruction provides a way to systematically structure the needed changes from classroom to boardroom to prepare students to leave our schools with the academic skills needed to be both career and college ready. It is more than an approach to enhancing instruction and instructional capacity. It is a way of thinking about what we believe about children, schools, and learning, which has coalesced at a critical time in American education. It is a way of thinking about standards, assessments, accountability, and teacher evaluation systems that are aligned with budgets, and show awareness of the global economy, technological innovation, "wired kids," and public policy debates.

DSEI builds on the ideas, inspirations, practices, and research of others, including the best research and meta-analysis on effective instruction and rigorous learning. It also builds on years of collective experience that International Center staff, consultants, and thought leaders have accumulated from thousands of American schools. The system recognizes the primacy and immeasurable value of great teachers and great teaching and strives to align education systems and functions with what teachers need to be to best support students. It does so by looking not only at teachers, but also beyond the classroom to inspire leadership at all levels in support of instruction. DSEI challenges all educators to consider the possible with a sense of practical urgency and a buoyant sense of the possible.

DSEI is a way to transform a traditional system into one that better supports all teachers and therefore more fully prepares every student for college, careers, and citizenship.

Systemwide Shifts in Thinking and Action

DSEI is designed to encourage and enable twenty-first-century districts and schools through twenty-first-century thinking and doing. This means it is also designed to steer you and your teams away from outdated thinking that will leave you stuck in the twentieth-century way of doing things.

The following comparison charts are useful checks to ensure that as you put the elements of DSEI into place, you are shifting your thinking to that which will drive successful, twenty-first-century actions and decisions. The left-hand column represents outmoded/traditional thinking and doing. The right-hand column represents the twenty-first-century, DSEI-aligned way of thinking and doing.

Use these shifts as guides as you discuss, plan, and implement DSEI.

Organizational Leadership Shifts

Traditional System	Daggett System
Set vision by top leadership	Set vision with wide contributions
Define vision in few academic measures	Define vision in terms of whole student needs
Place priority on short-term results	Place priority on long-term improvement
Limit goals to best students	Expand goals to all students
See vision as top leaders' initiative	Embrace vision universally
Instill fear with goals	Inspire passion with goals
Rigid structure to support adult needs	Flexible structure to support student needs
Top-down change for ease of administration/compliance—teachers as objects of change	Top-down support for bottom-up reform—teachers as agents of change

Instructional Leadership Shifts

Traditional System	Daggett System
Manage in the current system	Change the system
Use past experience to solve problems	Learn new ways to adapt and change
Promote standard procedures	Adapt to unique situations
Replicate practices with fidelity	Create new practices to meet student needs
Look to supervisors for answers	Look to staff to take actions
Rely on individual expertise	Share each other's expertise
Authority	Collaboration

Teaching Shifts

Traditional System	Daggett System
Teaching-focused	Learning-focused
Time-based	Learn new ways to adapt and change
Subject-driven	Interdisciplinary
Routine	Varied
High expectations for knowledge acquisition	High expectations for application of knowledge

Appendix

References

Chapter One

Frey, Carl, & and Osborne, Michael (2013). The Future of Employment: How Susceptible Are Jobs to Computerisation? Oxford, UK: University of Oxford. http://www.oxfordmartin.ox.ac.uk/downloads/academic/The_Future_of_Employment.pdf

Irwin, Neil (2015). Why very low interest rates may stick around. *New York Times*, December 14, 2015. http://www.nytimes.com/2015/12/15/upshot/why-very-low-interest-rates-may-stick-around.html?_r=0

Pew Research Center (2015). The American middle class is losing ground. http://www.pewsocialtrends.org/2015/12/09/the-american-middle-class-is-losing-ground/

Satterfield, Dee (2015). There's never been a better time to invest in tech. Here's why. Bonner & Partners. https://bonnerandpartners.com/theres-never-been-a-better-time-to-invest-in-tech-heres-why/

Chapter Two

Bandura, Albert (1977). "Self-Efficacy: Toward a Unifying Theory of Behavioral Change." *Psychological Review* 84 (2): 191–215. http://citeseerx.ist.psu.edu/viewdoc/download?doi=10.1.1.315.4567&rep=rep1&type=pdf

Ortman, Jennifer, Velkoff, Victoria, & Hogan, Howard (2014). An aging nation: The older population in the United States. Washington, D.C., U.S. Census Bureau. https://www.census.gov/prod/2014pubs/p25-1140.pdf

U.S. Census Bureau (2011). New Quick Facts, January 7, 2011. https://www.census.gov/quickfacts/table/PST045215/00

Chapter Three

American Institutes for Research (2012). Big gaps in earnings for Tennessee college grads. http://www.air.org/news/press-release/big-gaps-earnings-tennessee-college-grads

Brandon, Emily (2014). Workplace benefits that are disappearing. *U.S. News &World Report/Money*, July 28, 2014. http://money.usnews.com/money/retirement/articles/2014/07/28/workplace-benefits-that-are-disappearing

Career Readiness Partner Council (2015). What it means to be career ready. http://careerreadynow.org/docs/CRPC_4pagerB.pdf

Cowen, Tyler (2004). *Creative Destruction: How Globalization Is Changing the World's Cultures.* Princeton, NJ: Princeton University Press.

Craver, Jack (2015). Companies focusing less on traditional benefits. BenefitsPRO.com. http://www.benefitspro.com/2015/07/27/companies-focusing-less-on-traditional-benefits?&slreturn=1474321029

Experience.com (2016). Career statistics. https://www.experience.com/alumnus/article?channel_id=career_management&source_page=additional_articles&article_id=article_1247505066959

IFEBP.org (2014). Companies offering innovative benefits to attract millennial workforce. http://www.ifebp.org/aboutus/pressroom/releases/Pages/pr_120914.aspx

Pennington, Maura (2013). Millennials seek 21st century careers with 20th century skills. *Forbes*, October 22, 2013. http://www.forbes.com/sites/maurapennington/2013/10/22/millennials-seek-21st-century-careers-with-20th-century-skills/#133305912052

Terhune, Chad (2013). Part-timers to lose pay amid health act's new math. *Los Angeles Times,* May 2, 2013. http://articles.latimes.com/2013/may/02/business/la-fi-part-time-healthcare-20130502

U.S. Bureau of Labor Statistics (2015). FAQs about national longitudinal surveys. http://www.bls.gov/nls/nlsfaqs.htm

Wagner, Tony (2015). *Most Likely to Succeed: Preparing Our Kids for the Innovation Era.* New York: Scribner.

Weissman, Jordan (2012). 53% of recent college grads are jobless or underemployed—How? *The Atlantic,* April 23, 2012. http://www.theatlantic.com/business/archive/2012/04/53-of-recent-college-grads-are-jobless-or-underemployed-how/256237/

Chapter Four

Weber, Jeff (2015). What employers really want from millennials. http://www.eremedia.com/tlnt/what-employers-really-want-from-millennials/

Chapter Five

Bornstein, David (2015). Teaching social skills to improve grades and lives. *New York Times*, July 24, 2015. http://opinionator.blogs.nytimes.com/2015/07/24/building-social-skills-to-do-well-in-math/?_r=3

Harvard Graduate School of Education (2014). Creating pathways to prosperity: A blueprint for action. http://www.agi.harvard.edu/pathways/CreatingPathwaystoProsperityReport2014.pdf

International Center for Leadership in Education (2007). *Personal Skill Development in Grades 6–12*. Rexford, NY: International Center for Leadership in Education.

Robert Wood Johnson Foundation (2015). How children's social competence impacts their well-being in adulthood. http://www.rwjf.org/en/library/research/2015/07/how-children-s-social-competence-impacts-their-well-being-in-adu.html

Chapter Six

ActionCoach (2016). Twelve essential characteristics of an entrepreneur. http://www.actioncoach.com/_downloads/whitepaper-FranchiseRep5.pdf

Della Cava, Marco (2014). How Facebook changed our lives. *USA Today*, February 2, 2014. http://www.usatoday.com/story/tech/2014/02/02/facebook-turns-10-cultural-impact/5063979/

Demos, Telis (2015). Airbnb raises $1.5 billion in one of largest private placements. *Wall Street Journal*, June 26, 2015. http://www.wsj.com/articles/airbnb-raises-1-5-billion-in-one-of-largest-private-placements-1435363506?mod=LS1

Intuit (2007). Intuit future of small business report. http://http-download.intuit.com/http.intuit/CMO/intuit/futureofsmallbusiness/SR-1037_intuit_SmallBiz_Demog.pdf

LaJoie, Marc, & Shearman, Nick (2015). What is Alibaba? *Wall Street Journal.* http://projects.wsj.com/alibaba/

Mudallal, Zainab (2015). Airbnb will soon be booking more rooms than the world's largest hotel chains. Quartz.com, January 20, 2015. http://qz.com/329735/airbnb-will-soon-be-booking-more-rooms-than-the-worlds-largest-hotel-chains/

Pink, Daniel (2002). *Free Agent Nation: The Future of Working for Yourself.* New York: Business Plus.

Small Business and Entrepreneurship Council (2016). Small business facts. http://sbecouncil.org/about-us/facts-and-data/

Chapter Seven

Investopedia (2016). Zero-based budgeting—ZBB. http://www.investopedia.com/terms/z/zbb.asp

Spring Branch ISD (2015). Things to know about the Districts of Innovation Opportunity in SBISD. https://www.springbranchisd.com/innovation/

Taboada, Melissa (2016). Dripping Springs district among first in Texas to get innovation tag. *Austin American Statesman*, August 18, 2016. http://www.mystatesman.com/news/news/local/dripping-springs-district-among-first-in-texas-to-/nsHM7/

Chapter Eight

Bureau of Labor Statistics, U.S. Department of Labor (2016). *Occupational Outlook Handbook, 2016-17 Edition.* http://www.bls.gov/ooh/architecture-and-engineering/cartographers-and-photogrammetrists.htm

Chui, Michael, Manyika, James, & Miremadi, Mehdi (2015). Four fundamentals of workplace automation. McKinsey & Company, November 2015. http://www.mckinsey.com/business-functions/business-technology/our-insights/four-fundamentals-of-workplace-automation

Dishman, Lydia (2016a). These are the top 25 jobs in the U.S. this year. FastCompany.com, January 11, 2016. https://www.fastcompany.com/3055629/the-future-of-work/these-are-the-top-25-jobs-in-the-us-this-year

Dishman, Lydia (2016b). How to satisfy demand for the biggest job of the 21st century. FastCompany.com, April 1, 2016. http://www.fastcompany.com/3058502/the-future-of-work/how-to-satisfy-demand-for-the-biggest-job-of-the-21st-century

Frey, Carl, & Osborne, Michael (2013). The future of employment: How susceptible are jobs to computerization? Oxford, UK: University of Oxford. http://www.oxfordmartin.ox.ac.uk/downloads/academic/The_Future_of_Employment.pdf

Hahn, Jason (2016). Pew: 65 percent of Americans expect robots to take their work within 50 years. Digitaltrends.com, March 13, 2016. http://www.digitaltrends.com/cool-tech/pew-robots-job-threats/#:zKZ5rsH3NhS57A

IBISWorld (2016). Auto mechanics in the US: Market research report. IBISWorld, April 2016. http://www.ibisworld.com/industry/default.aspx?indid=1689

Leubsdorf, Ben (2016). The hurdles to getting U.S. workers off the sidelines. *Wall Street Journal*, March 6, 2016. http://www.wsj.com/articles/the-hurdles-to-getting-u-s-workers-off-the-sidelines-1457292446

Lieberman, Mark (2015). 10 disappearing middle-class jobs. MSN Money, March 17, 2015. http://www.msn.com/en-us/money/generalmoney/10-disappearing-middle-class-jobs/ss-AA9QncX

McGonigal, Jane (2016). *Reality Is Broken: Why Games Make Us Better and How They Can Change the World*. New York: Penguin Press, 2011.

My Private Banking (2016). Hybrid robos will manage 10% of investable assets by 2025. MyPrivateBanking.com, February 11, 2016. http://www.myprivatebanking.com/article/report-hybrid-robo-advisors-2016

Wissinger, Chrissy (2011). Smartphones and tablets replacing alarm clocks, GPS devices & digital cameras, according to mobile survey. Prosper Mobile Insights, July 6, 2011. http://www.prweb.com/releases/2011/7/prweb8620690.htm

Chapter Ten

Council of Chief State School Officers (CCSSO) (2011). *InTASC Model Core Teaching Standards: A Resource for State Dialogue*. file:///C:/Users/Robert.Robert-PC/Downloads/intasc_model_core_teaching_standards_2011.pdf

Danielson, Charlotte (2007). *Enhancing Professional Practice: A Framework for Teaching*. Princeton, NJ: The Danielson Group. www.danielsongroup.org/theframeteach.htm

Hattie, John (2008). *Visible Learning: A Synthesis of Over 800 Meta-Analyses Relating to Achievement*. London: Routledge.

Higgins, Steve, Kokotsaki, Dimitra, & Coe, Robert (2011). Sutton Trust toolkit of strategies to improve learning. Durham University, Durham, UK. http://www.letterboxclub.org.uk/usr/library/documents/main/toolkit-of-strategies-spending-pp.pdf

Lucey, Linda, Silver, Doug, Corso, Mickey, & Fox, Kristine (2010). *Focused on Student Success: A Five-Year Research Study of Models, Networks, and Policies to Support and Sustain Rigor and Relevance for ALL Students.* Successful Practices Network. http://fea.spnetwork.org/spn/media/files/articles/research/FocusedOnStudentSuccess_7%2026.pdf

Marzano, Robert (2007). *The Art and Science of Teaching.* Alexandria, VA: Association for Supervision & Curriculum Development